MISSING IN RED

JUDY PARKINSON

DEDICATION

For Warren, John, and Lisa with love

Also, by Judy Parkinson

Crystal

AN UNUSUAL ALLIANCE

Missing In Red

ISBN: 9781876409036

CHAPTER 1
November 2021

Ellington puffs his way down a narrow lane. It's an unfamiliar place...dark, menacing, filthy. His legs feel like lead and he fights for breath. The overpowering stink of sewerage blended with the sour smell of urine envelopes him in a suffocating cloud. At the end of the lane, he sees a small group of people standing beneath a street light. The thud of fast approaching footsteps shoots ice through his veins. He stops and listens. The noise seems all around him. Is it in front or behind? A huge dark shape materialises out of the shadows, and an iron arm fastens around his neck and slams him hard against the wall. Although Ellington can't see the face, he knows who it is. He tries desperately to escape the vice-like grip, but his body is paralysed and he can't move a muscle. He tries to shout 'help' but all that comes from his mouth is a hoarse squeak. A knife hovers above his throat. He squeaks again as it swishes down.

An irritating noise rattles his brain. As the sound crescendos, the blackness dissolves and Ellington wakes with the squeak still trapped in his throat. The alarm clock continues its persistent beeping. Shivering with shock, Ellington finally silences it with an open palm.

He lies stiffly in bed recovering from the nightmare, his

heart pounding and his mouth dry. A pain settles in the front of his skull. He turns over, groans and reaches for the glass of water on the bedside table. The taste in his mouth reminds him of the six or more neat scotches he'd quaffed the previous night, the drinks he'd downed in a fit of maudlin, the sad mood that started on the drive home, driven by thoughts of past loves and what might have been. The sun streams through the louvres splashing pale stripes across the ruffled sheets, the sheets that had soaked up the sweat he'd shed during the night, courtesy of the ghastly dream.

It takes five minutes before Ellington can gather the impetus to tumble out of bed and head for the bathroom. He stands under the steaming water allowing it to turn his skin pink, hoping the heat will somehow release him from the aftermath of the dream, the dream that recurs again and again, the dream that began its torment four months ago.

*

The Station, on the southern fringe of the city, is one of the biggest and busiest in the metropolitan area. The main room comprises a sea of desks and filing cabinets, separated from each other by narrow walkways. Only Chief Inspector Bellamy has a private office, and while no one can see through the black glass surrounding him, Bellamy has a bird's eye view of his entire staff. A huge whiteboard is mounted on the end wall, and other paraphernalia is grouped around it. Fluorescent lighting creates a harsh brightness, and the air conditioning is always set too cold. Sergeant Geoff Murray is in charge of the temperature and although everyone grumbles, no one ever challenges him.

Ellington is no sooner at his desk when Bellamy strides over. Ellington smells his boss before he sees him. The cheap cologne Bellamy likes to drown in, spreads in all directions.

Ellington estimates his boss to be around sixty. Early photos show him handsome, lean and fit. Now the face, along with the body has grown coarse. Bellamy's one redeeming feature is the full thatch of perfectly groomed sandy hair which seems at odds with the rest of him. Ellington often wonders if it's a hairpiece.

'A missing person report came in during the night, young woman didn't come home, completely out of character. The parents reported it around two.' Bellamy throws a thin file onto the desk.

Ellington is immediately hit with a wallop of déjà vu. Most of those words were the same words used by the same man in this same place over a year ago. He opens the file dismissing the disturbing thoughts that are trying to invade his mind. He looks at the file and frowns. 'She's been missing less than a day.'

'Officially missing since yesterday morning,' Bellamy growls.

'She's from Summer Hill. Why aren't the Summer Hill guys looking after it?' Ellington asks.

'It's been sent to us, specifically for you.'

'I don't get it, why me?'

'You've made a name for yourself Duke. Catching Clarence Campbell was no mean feat.' Bellamy prods the file with an index finger. 'Upstairs has ordered priority.'

Ellington's eyebrows shoot up. He knows what Bellamy means by 'upstairs', someone well up in the pecking order. Top brass. He glances again at the open file. 'David Seymour is the father of the missing girl. That name rings a bell.'

'It should, he's an independent in Parliament.'

'Oh,' Ellington mutters hoping his cynicism isn't showing.

'Take Bradley,' Bellamy orders.

'The rookie?'

'You obviously don't take notice of your colleagues' stripes. She's just been promoted to senior constable, hardly a rookie. I'd say more like a smart cookie.'

They both look over in Sarah Bradley's direction. She's looking straight at them but quickly turns back to her computer.

'The parents are anxious, don't make them wait.'

'What about the Gallego case? We're closing in.'

'Murray can take over, he's across it.'

'But....'

'No buts,' Bellamy barks as he stomps back to his office.

Ellington drops the folder into his briefcase, grabs his jacket and crosses to Sarah Bradley's desk. In the three weeks since the girl started at the station, Ellington has not passed a single word with her apart from a distant *good morning*. He notices her straight back and slender shoulders as she taps into her computer. She's small and slim, with a face so young and innocent she could still be at school in the tenth grade. Her silky honey-coloured hair is pulled back into a tight bun low on the nape of her neck. She senses Ellington's presence and looks up with wide, blue eyes. This is probably the closest she's been to the man who has fascinated her from day one, a man who effortlessly exudes an aura of authority and elegance more suited perhaps to a university professor than a policeman... the man they call Duke. In that instant, Sarah notes the wavy crop of dark hair slightly tinged with auburn, the deep-set blue eyes, the fine features, and strong square jaw. His shirt sleeves are rolled up to just under the elbow and his nondescript tie has been loosened beneath the top open button of his pale blue shirt. His jacket is slung over his shoulder, and he's carrying a worn leather briefcase.

'Get your hat Constable, you're on an assignment.' His tone is curt, he feels justifiably irritated because some big shot put out an order, and now instead of doing something useful like catching a murderer, he's sent to look for some stupid, rich kid who didn't come home because she got stoned and passed out in someone's pad. Well at least that's what he hopes has happened to Elise Seymour.

Sarah stumbles after Ellington as he races down the stairs to the dingy basement car park. She can feel the adrenalin pumping through her. An assignment with the Duke? Her heart is racing and her mind spinning. A mass of nervous tension, she sits beside him and fumbles with the safety belt. He spends a few seconds tapping the address into his navigator before putting the car into motion.

They sit in silence as they drive out of the city and head down Parramatta Road. The thoughts of that other missing persons case fifteen months ago, are crowding Ellington's mind. As the memories take root, he finds himself silently praying that this present case will not carry any of the same horrors.

CHAPTER 2
August 2020

'A missing person report just came in...young woman didn't come home last night, completely out of character. Name's Melanie Churchill, lives in Glebe. I want you to interview the parents.' Bellamy growled as his phone started buzzing. He answered with a curt 'Yes?' Ellington watched as Bellamy's lips tightened and his jaw clenched. 'Yes, got that. Where did you say?' he scribbled on his desk pad. 'Witnesses?' He nodded and scribbled again. 'Called forensics?' He nodded again. 'We'll be there soon.' Bellamy looked up at Ellington. 'The body of a young woman has just been found...an unoccupied warehouse in Redfern. I'll be sending Salerno, Farrugia, Pascoe and Bonnington. I want you to take control, set up a crime scene. The guy who found the body is still there. Bring him in if necessary. Forensic has been called and they're on their way.'

*

The area was semi-industrial with factories and workshops lining one side of the road and dilapidated fibro houses on the other. The late afternoon winter sun was shedding its final feeble rays as Ellington drove slowly along the road. Two police cars had parked in a no-parking zone, and three uniformed police were walking towards the warehouse. A Government forensic car was parked in front of the building's entrance. Ellington couldn't find a legal spot and parked in a driveway on the residential side. As he crossed the road, the icy wind that had blown up overnight swirled around him. He pulled his coat collar up around his ears and shoved both hands into his trouser pockets.

Inside the building, the forensic people were already at work. Both were wearing full white plastic regalia. One was taking photos and the other was kneeling beside the body which was lying face up in the middle of the area. Tony Salerno was questioning a scruffy elderly man. Ellington approached them.

Salerno spoke: 'This gentleman found the body.'

Ellington nodded. 'Your name sir?'

'Ed Duncan. I found her just before I called Emergency.'

'And how come you were in this building? I understand it's been closed and unused for some months.'

The man hesitated, blinked his eyes, and ran a gnarled hand around the back of his neck. 'Well, a mate of mine was squatting here a week or so back and he invited me in for a drink. He had a key and showed me where it was kept if I needed a squat sometime. He hid the key behind a loose brick near the front entrance.'

'And when you entered the building, it would have been......what time?'

'Around three.'

'And apart from the deceased, was anyone else here?'

'No, only her. Jesus, how could anybody do that?' The man glanced toward the dead woman. Ellington followed his gaze. One of the forensic people was now using tiny tweezers to extract something from the woman's hair. The contents were carefully placed into a glass phial.

'No sign of anyone else'?

'No sir.'

'Before today, when was the last time you were here?' Ellington asked.

The man hesitated and rubbed his neck again. 'Yesterday. I'd slept here the night before and left around ten yesterday morning. I didn't sleep here last night.'

'And when you left here Wednesday morning, there was no one around, nothing out of the ordinary?'

'No sir.' The man's eyes darted around the room. 'I've got some things here, a blanket, some food.'

'Get them and let Constable Salerno check them. Give him the key and all your details before you go. This area is being cordoned off, so don't come back.' As the man turned to go, Ellington held up his hand. 'No, hold on, we'll need to get a DNA sample. Stay around. The forensic people will organise that.'

Ellington's eyes swept around the area and settled on Constables Farrugia, Pascoe and Bonnington standing near the front entrance. 'Tape all around the front of the building,' he shouted.

Followed by Salerno, Ellington walked towards the body. He flinched at the sight of the naked victim. Salerno stood by quietly, desperately trying to subdue the bile growling in his stomach. Admitting defeat, he made a hurried exit from the building.

The sight was truly horrendous. One of the woman's eyes was missing, there was caked blood all around her mouth and there was a gaping bloody hole where her left breast once was. There were other deep wounds on her abdomen.

The forensic person who had been taking samples stood and faced Ellington. He was surprised to be looking into a pair of liquid brown eyes framed by perfectly shaped black eyebrows.

'Can you assess the time of death?' Ellington asked.

'Twelve to sixteen hours ago. I will have a more accurate time at the autopsy' The woman spoke with a slight accent.

'Cause of death?' Ellington asked.

'Multiple wounds…any one of them could have caused death. Again, the autopsy will reveal all.' As she spoke, the woman dragged off her mask and threw back the plastic hood, revealing a beautiful face. The high sculptured cheekbones were enhanced by a flawless olive complexion and perfect features.

'The person who did this is a monster. There are teeth marks in the eye socket. It appears the eye was eaten out.'

'Oh God,' Ellington muttered.

'And the missing breast. There are teeth marks there too. Part of her tongue is also missing.'

'When will you do the autopsy?'

'Maybe tonight, maybe tomorrow.'

'I'd appreciate your sending me the results Dr…?' Ellington handed the girl his card.

'Mirrakoff. Ivana Mirrakoff.'

Ellington found Salerno leaning against the door of the car, his face deathly pale.

'Sorry, Sarge. I don't know what came over me.'

'It's called squeamish Sal. It happens to almost every cop once. You've had yours. It won't happen again.'

Back at the station, Ellington filled in time looking up unsolved murders in and around the area. When Ivana hadn't phoned by eight, he headed home.

He zapped some left-over patties in the microwave and pulled a beer from the fridge. The beer was gone in five minutes and he grabbed another. One look at the patties told him he wasn't hungry. He tossed them in the kitchen tidy and drained his second bottle. Reluctantly he allowed himself to think about the murder and its time frame. Ed Duncan had left the squat at ten Wednesday morning and returned around three Thursday. The killer brought the girl to the warehouse sometime after ten Wednesday morning. But why a warehouse surrounded by factories and houses? Wouldn't a place out in the bush be more appropriate?

Ivana didn't call until late the following day. Her soft accented voice told it all: 'The woman was killed around three Thursday morning. Cause of death, choking. But the terrible carnage on her body was an associated cause. She had sustained a hefty blow to the skull which could have caused unconsciousness. Her left eye had been extracted by human teeth and half her tongue by a sharp knife. The left breast had been partly bitten and partly removed by the knife. Knife wounds were also present on her abdomen and genital area. She had been raped.'

'Was she killed in the warehouse?'

'Blood patterns are consistent with that.'

'DNA?'

'Yes. We have some good samples. There was semen and saliva on the body, and fresh blood in the storeroom.'

'Storeroom?'

'It's likely the suspect was disturbed when the squatter arrived and escaped through the storeroom window. The window had been damaged. and he was cut by some glass slivers.'

The next afternoon Ivana phoned again. 'We were lucky with the DNA. The suspect's blood group is quite rare. Normally DNA matching can take a week or more, but not in this case.'

*

'The collected samples belong to a man named Clarence Campbell who'd been tried and acquitted of a murder five years ago. The murder had the same trademarks as this one, gruesome, sadistic.' Ellington threw Ivana's report onto Bellamy's desk.

'I remember the case. The bloke's a bit of an enigma. He owned valuable property all over the State, had enough money to pay one of the most expensive barristers in the country. He ran a brothel for a few years but that would only account for some of his wealth. We strongly suspect that drug trading was involved.'

'How do we find him?'

'With difficulty. Another murder a year or so ago looked like Campbell's work. Although the DNA was destroyed by fire, other aspects of the crime pointed to Campbell. But we couldn't find him, seemed to have disappeared into thin air.'

'What about his numerous properties?'

'He sold them all. We spoke to the various purchasers…all just ordinary people looking for a house. The agent handling the deals was kept in the dark. Everything was done by phone, and money was deposited online from accounts that were closed after each deal. He opened a new account each time.'

'Banks need all sorts of ID before they open accounts. They also need addresses.'

'He satisfied them, showed his driver's licence, Medicare card, birth certificate, everything else they wanted. Apparently, the addresses he gave were never properly checked, they were all bogus. But he'd never had a conviction and that helped him pull the wool.'

'So, we start searching again. This time for real.'

'It was for real last time. We hit a dead end.'

'I guess we start with his associates. Got a list?'

'That's another problem, there are no records of associates.'

'Relatives?'

'He had a wife.'

'Had?'

'She's still alive, but hiding away somewhere. She'll be just as hard to find as him. She's terrified of him, changed her appearance and vanished.'

'Kids? Siblings?

'No kids. Two brothers. Maybe they're still at the same addresses.'

*

The house was in Penrith, a suburb which not all that many years ago was a country town west of the city. But it wasn't long before the town was thriving and attracting huge numbers of settlers taking advantage of the affordable housing.

Gary Noonan's house was a neat house on a neat street. There was a ubiquitous feeling about the area. All the houses had timber cladding, Colourbond roofs, small front verandas and orderly gardens. Gum trees grew along the nature strips with colourful flowers blooming at their bases.

The door was opened by a tall, heavily built middle-aged man. He wore a short greying beard and moustache along with a grubby white tee and a pair of stubby shorts. He squinted at Ellington through narrow eyes. Ellington flipped open his ID and introduced himself. 'Detective Luke Ellington. I'd like to talk with Gary Noonan?'

'That's me. It's about Clarrie I suppose. Come in.'

Ellington followed the man through a narrow hall into what appeared to be a family room. Newspapers were spread over the floor and the television was blaring. Noonan turned it off and pointed to a chair. He sat opposite. While still standing, Ellington asked: 'When did you last see your brother, Clarence Campbell?'

'Campbell isn't my brother. I was eight years old before I ever laid eyes on him.'

'Our records show he was your sibling.'

'No way,' the man scoffed. 'Three years after my dad died, mum met this guy at the club…George Campbell. He moved into the house and after a few months started talking about his son who was in foster care. Mum agreed to take the kid in. She even adopted him.'

'How did you react to that?'

'He was thirteen, five years older than me. I hated him. He was a bully and he made my life hell. I complained to mum, but she was under George's thumb. He was a controlling bastard.'

'What about your brother?'

'Callum? Poor little kid. He was only five when Campbell came…terrified of the fucker.'

'What happened while Campbell was living with you?'

'It was hell…but it only lasted three years. He was gone soon after he turned sixteen.'

'How was it hell?'

'He tortured things, cats, frogs. I caught him one day with Cal. He had him tied up to a tree stump, and was sticking lit cigarettes on his bum. I picked up a rock and threw it at him and then I went screaming to the next-door neighbour.'

'What happened then?'

'The neighbour came and got Cal free and took us to his place. Then when mum came home, he told her what had happened. Mum thanked him and said she would look after it. But she never did. She never said a thing to Clarrie or to

George. But she did make sure she never left either of us alone ever again with the creep.'

'After Campbell left, what happened with the family?'

'Mum and George just carried on like nothing had ever happened.'

'And you and Callum?'

'I did my School Certificate and took on a plumbing trade. That's what I do now. I work for a company, I get a wage, I've got a wife and two daughters and I'm satisfied with my life.'

'And Callum?'

Gary's face crumpled a little and he closed his eyes. 'Poor bastard. He never really got over having to live in the same house as Clarrie and copping all that cruelty. When he was fifteen, Cal became mentally unstable, started hearing voices. He never recovered. He's living in a hostel for the mentally ill. He's on medication that's turned him into a zombie. He doesn't know me.' Gary wiped a large hairy hand over his wet eyes and gave a little sob.

'I'm sorry. What happened to your mother....and George?'

'Both dead. George died of cancer of the lungs around the same time I finished school, and mum died a few years later with breast cancer.'

'Did you ever meet Campbell's wife?'

'No. I only heard at that trial that he had a wife...poor woman.'

*

Ellington decided interviewing Callum would be a waste of time and headed back to Sydney. He was greeted by Bellamy. 'The body in the warehouse has been identified...the girl reported missing, Melanie Churchill. She left work around six and never made it to her car parked two blocks away.' Bellamy's frown deepened and his mouth settled into a hard straight line. 'I didn't know how long you'd be gone so I sent Murray to interview the parents.'

'I'd like to know more about Campbell's trial... the one five years ago. Do we have a transcript?' Ellington asked.

'Should be one in the file'.

*

Ellington spent the following day reading the transcripts of Campbell's trial. There was a lot to read as the trial had been lengthy. A covering letter came with the transcripts.

The victim had been missing for two days before being found in bushland. The body had been badly burned and any available DNA had been destroyed. A witness testified he had seen a man dragging what looked to be a body from a car into the area. A car later passed him as he drove home. The witness was sure it was the same car that was parked near the crime scene. He recorded the vehicle's number plate and this led to Campbell's arrest. The defence questioned the man's ability to accurately identify Campbell owing to the lack of light. They also severely criticised his ability to accurately record a number plate while driving and asked why had he not recorded the number plate when he first witnessed the crime. The witness was later found to be suffering from a form of epilepsy which threw further doubt on his testimony. And then when it seemed both sides had finished giving their evidence, two witnesses came forward. These testimonies threw enough doubt to convince the jury to bring in a 'not guilty verdict.

Ellington read the testimonies over and over. One of the witnesses was a prostitute who called herself Tiffany Spice. She testified that on the night of the murder, Campbell had engaged her for sex. During the encounter, Campbell became rough and abusive. When he threatened her with a knife, she escaped to her front room and screamed. A friend passing by heard her screams, rushed in, disarmed Campbell and bludgeoned him with a baseball bat. The man stayed with Tiffany that night and in his evidence, swore that Campbell didn't regain consciousness until morning.

Ellington shook his head and muttered to himself: 'So, a friend just happened to be passing by at the exact time of the murder, he just happened to be carrying a baseball bat and just happened to disarm this dangerous and experienced thug.' What sort of testimonies were those? They stunk to high heaven. He took note of the defence barrister and decided to pay him a visit first thing Monday.

*

The chambers of Nigel Wymark were in one of the prestigious law buildings near the Phillip Street Courts. Wymark was a short, round man in his late sixties. Thick white hair matched a trim white moustache. His impeccable dark suit was set off with a mustard-coloured waistcoat and matching tie. His chambers reflected the style of the early twentieth century...ornate ceilings, antique lights, walnut panelling and heavy velvet curtains. One wall was entirely covered with books and another with expensive oil paintings. An enormous highly polished mahogany desk stood beside the window wall. A peculiar but not unpleasant aroma hung in the air...something like a combination of scotch whisky and furniture polish. Wymark greeted Ellington with a firm handshake.

He spoke with an elite accent. 'As I explained on the phone detective, I'm squeezing you in between clients, so only have,' he glanced at his watch, 'fifteen minutes.'

'I'll try to be quick. I'm interested in a case you defended five years ago...Clarence Campbell. He was acquitted of a murder charge. You recall the case?'

Wymark plonked onto the chair behind his desk and

pointed at the one opposite. He tapped his forehead. 'Yes, I do remember. Quite a nasty murder as I recall.'

'I am presently investigating a similar murder. Last week, a young woman was brutally and sadistically killed. DNA belonging to Clarence Campbell was all over her body. It's vital he's found.'

'I don't know how I can help.'

'Before and during the trial, did Campbell ever mention close associates or friends?'

'He had a couple of stepbrothers. But they didn't get involved. I think there was a lot of bad feeling there. But associates, friends? He never mentioned anyone.'

'The witnesses, Tiffany Spice and her friend Vince Mowbray gave evidence that tipped the scales. I read the court transcript and found their evidence rather unbelievable.'

'Well, it convinced the jury. They obviously didn't find it unbelievable.'

'How did you come to take on the defence?'

'Campbell approached me. He had done his homework and read of my various successes. I explained my costs and without hesitation, he agreed to them.'

'A witness testified he saw Campbell drag a body into the bush. How did he get off?'

'If you read the court transcript you would have seen that the witness was discredited.'

'Did you think Campbell was innocent?'

'It's not my job to decide that. It's for the jury. Everyone deserves a defence.'

'When those two witnesses gave their testimonies, how did the Prosecutor react?'

'He treated them like a joke.'

'I can't believe he didn't tear shreds out of them. I assume he had plenty of time to prepare a decent cross-examination?'

Wymark coughed softly. 'Well, that evidence came a bit late in the piece. We didn't include it in our initial Submissions.'

'How long did the Prosecution have to work with it?'

'Around two weeks, if I remember correctly.'

'That all?'

'He could have asked for an extension but didn't. He did his best to ridicule them and obviously thought the jury would disregard their testimonies. But of course, that didn't happen.'

'I would like to talk with Miss Spice and Mowbray. Do you have any addresses, contact numbers?'

'There could be something in the file. I'll get my clerk to look it up for you. If you'd like to wait in the front office, Miss Purcell will look after you.'

Miss Purcell was a short birdlike woman with cropped brown hair, rimless glasses, and a permanent frown. 'Tiffany Spice lived in Darlinghurst at the time of the trial. I have an address but of course, she may not be still there.' She handed Ellington a sheet of notepaper. 'There's a mobile number too.'

'Thank you. Anything on Mowbray?'

'The only particulars he gave were the same as Miss Spice's.'

'They lived together?'

'He gave that impression but I don't think so. He was her pimp.'

'Did she work from a brothel?'

'Apparently not. If my memory serves me right, all her engagements were conducted in her home.'

Out in the street, Ellington called the number. A low husky voice asked the caller to leave a message. Ellington checked the address and made for the carpark.

The street in Darlinghurst was packed with rows of two-story fully-attached terraces. Some dated back to the early twentieth century, some maybe even before that, most were dilapidated. Tiffany Spice's terrace was badly run down. A short cracked concrete pathway ran through an overgrown weedy front yard. Ellington pounded on the brass knocker and waited patiently.

A voice sounded from above. 'The business is closed. Go away.'

Ellington looked up and saw a tousled blonde head hanging over the balustrade of the narrow balcony.

'Are you Tiffany?' Ellington shouted.

'No, I'm the Queen of Sheba,'. she yelled.

'Detective Sergeant Ellington'. He held up his ID.

'I'm registered. You've got nothing on me.'

'I know. I'm not here to harass you. I just have to ask you some questions. It could save someone's life.' Ellington hoped this might appeal to her better nature.

'Hang on.'

A few moments later, the door opened. Tiffany wore a black see-through negligee over black underwear.

'Watcha want?' she asked, chewing furiously on a wad of gum.

'Could I come in?'

'Let's see that ID again.'

Ellington flipped open his ID wallet.

'Okay, come in.' She tossed her head to one side and held the door open. He passed in front of her and entered the small front room. Tiffany closed the door and faced him.

'Well, Sergeant Pepper?'

'I'm trying to find the person who killed a young woman last Thursday.' Ellington looked Tiffany up and down and added: 'She'd have been around your age.'

'What could I know?'

'I think you might know the person who did it.'

The girl's expression remained unchanged. Ellington continued. 'It was Clarence Campbell.' Ellington noted the girl's eyes widening.

'I haven't seen the fucker since that day in court.'

'I believe you. But I have a feeling you could tell me where he might be.'

'I don't have a clue.'

'You lied for him five years ago and so did your mate Mowbray. Campbell's a very dangerous man. Are you still lying for him?'

'Vince knew Campbell, I'd never met him before.'

'Where's Vince now?'

'In gaol. That's why I'm closing up my business and shooting through.'

'What's he in gaol for?'

'Drug dealing.'

'Which prison?'

'Silverwater.'

*

Vince Mowbray shuffled into the interrogation area of Silverwater Prison. The scrawny, rat-faced man, wearing prison overalls, stared insolently at Ellington.

'We're looking for Clarence Campbell and believe you might be able to assist.'

Mowbray sneered, showing crooked yellow teeth.

'What's in it for me? Why should I help you?'

'If you give us evidence that leads to Campbell's arrest, I will recommend that your sentence is reduced.'

Mowbray scratched his stubbly chin, raised his eyebrows and squinted at Ellington.

'Can I have that in writing?'

'That's not how it works. But I promise you, if you help

us capture Campbell, I will seek a reduction. Whether it's granted or not, is not in my arena. But having Campbell on the loose is a threat to society. He's a vicious, sadistic killer and no one's safe while he's at large. Knowing that, I think the authorities would be very likely to show their gratitude if you play a part in his capture.'

Mowbray ran a hand through his greasy hair. 'I'll think about it.'

'Mr Mowbray, there is no time for thinking. I need an answer and I need it now.'

'Okay, okay.' Mowbray squeezed his eyes shut and kept them closed as he spoke. 'I met Campbell about ten years ago. He owned a brothel at the Cross and was making money hand over fist. I was new to the job and trying to set up my own clientele. He paid me to lay off and leave the area to him. He not only gave me money but also a job. I procured for him and he paid me a bonus for each new girl.' Mowbray's eyes snapped open and he eyeballed Ellington. 'Then Campbell got into drug dealing and sold the business to me.'

'Where did he go?'

'He went up to Queensland for a while.'

'Where in Queensland?'

'Gold Coast.'

'That would have been when?'

Mowbray squinted his eyes in thought. Early '2016 'till mid-2017.'

Ellington scribbled into his notebook before asking: 'Who were his associates?'

There was a long pause before Mowbray answered: 'Before he went away, I met his accountant and after he came back, I saw a cop at his house. They're the only two I've ever seen.'

'What are their names?'.

'The accountant works in Parramatta. His name is Wilcox. Phillip Wilcox.'

'And the policeman?'

'Don't know. Never heard his name.'

'But you met him?'

'I saw him one day, by accident.'

'Accident?'

'Yeah, it was soon after Clarrie was acquitted of that killing. I called around to see him and the door was opened. I heard talking in the back room so I listened. The cop wasn't in uniform but he was telling Clarrie about some crime his precinct was involved in. He was giving Clarrie all sorts of advice about cop procedure. There's no doubt he was a cop.'

'What did he look like?'

'I didn't see his face, had his back to me. He was tall, skinny, balding. That's all I saw. I left.'

'Did Campbell know you'd been there?'

'I never told him.'

'So, he didn't know you'd seen the policeman?'

'No.'

'Nothing more you can tell me?'

'That's it.' Mowbray stood and walked toward the guard standing near the door. He turned, and pointed a finger at Ellington. 'You owe me,' he growled.

*

Inspector Bellamy was cursing and shouting when Ellington walked into his office. 'Where in hell's name have you been?'

'Chasing up the Churchill murder. Sorry I should have called.'

'Yes, you should have,' Bellamy spluttered. 'There's been another missing person…young woman, left her job at six last night and never made it home.'

'Same area?'

'Glebe, not all that far from where we think Melanie Churchill was abducted.'

'I've got some leads on Melanie's murder.'

'Tell me.'

'I read the transcript of Campbell's trial and visited his attorney, Nigel Wymark. It seems the prosecution blokes didn't do a very good job in court but were possibly deliberately misled by the defence. Wymark gave me the names of two of Campbell's witnesses. One, a prostitute calling herself Tiffany Spice and a pimp called Mowbray. I interviewed the girl and learned nothing other than Mowbray was in Silverwater doing time for drug offences. I interviewed him and he gave me more information, the name of Campbell's accountant and also a crooked cop involved with Campbell.'

'The cop's name?'

'He didn't know.'

'Well, that was a bit of useless information.'

'Maybe so. But he also told me that Campbell had moved to the Gold Coast in 2016 and stayed there a year or so.'

Bellamy scratched his head and pointed a finger. 'I seem to remember there were a couple of pretty hideous murders up there a few years ago. No charges, no suspects. Let me take a look.' He opened his computer and typed. Within a minute, the results were there. 'The bodies of two young women were found in dense bushland. Both bodies were burned but there was reasonable evidence they had been tortured and mutilated prior to death. Because of the intensity of the fire, no DNA survived and they remain unsolved murders.'

'I'd like to visit the accountant Phillip Wilcox, and see

what he has to say.'

'Take Salerno.'

'No need. It'll be just a routine chat.'

*

Phillip Wilcox's office was situated in a side street running off Church Street, Parramatta. Ellington showed his ID to the girl at the front desk.

'Mr Wilcox's got a client right now. Would you like to come back in, say twenty minutes?'

'I'll wait. I'm after some information about a client, Clarence Campbell.'

'I'm sure Mr Wilcox will be able to help you.'

When the client left Wilcox's office fifteen minutes later, Ellington walked in. unannounced. Wilcox was sitting at his desk rifling through papers. He looked up with a surprised frown as Ellington approached.

Ellington showed his ID. 'Detective-Sergeant Ellington, South Sydney. I'm here about one of your clients, Clarence Campbell.'

The man's face contorted as the frown deepened. 'Campbell? He's not a client anymore.'

'Can you tell me who looks after his accounts now?'

'Haven't a clue,' Wilcox was defensive.

'What's Campbell's address?'

'I disposed of all those files. I don't have that information.'

Years of dealing with criminals and their associates had endowed Ellington with super powers of observation. He knew Wilcox was lying. 'When your memory returns, contact me.' Ellington threw his card on the desk and stormed out. He crossed the road entered a coffee shop, made an order and called Bellamy. 'I'm certain Wilcox is lying. I think it would be worthwhile following him. See if he leads me somewhere.'

'Want some backup?'

'Not at this stage.'

'Okay, keep in touch.'

'Forty minutes and two flat whites later, he was rewarded. Wilcox emerged from the building dragging a small wheelie bag. Ellington followed him to the Council car park and watched him climb into a car parked less than ten metres away from his own. He followed Wilcox through the main street and out onto the highway. Darkness was falling rapidly allowing Ellington to keep close behind without being detected. Wilcox stuck to the highway until coming to the suburb of North Rocks where he took a left turn. Ellington followed as the BMW wound around several back streets before pulling up beside a substantial brick house. Ellington parked opposite and watched as Wilcox drove through the open gateway and up the driveway. He waited ten minutes before crossing to the house, and keeping within the deep shadows, stealthily crept up the driveway. Lights were blazing inside the back section of the house. Ellington approached cautiously and peered through a window. Inside, Wilcox was talking into a phone, the wheelie bag was propped on the floor beside him. The night was freezing and Ellington's feet felt like blocks of ice. He watched Wilcox pour a hefty measure of whisky and down it in one long draught. He then pulled two bulging files from the bag and sifted through them. Ellington felt sure the papers had something to do with Campbell, but getting into the house unseen and viewing them, was presenting an insurmountable problem. He was about to leave when a late model Mercedes came noisily up the driveway. He moved away from the house, hid in the doorway of the garden shed and watched. A large figure walked from the car, pounded on the back door and disappeared inside the house. Ellington then moved back to his position by the window and saw Wilcox hand the man the files.

At first Ellington could only see the back of the man, heavy build, broad shoulders. He couldn't hear any of the conversation, but Wilcox's expression showed fear. The man turned towards the door and in a flash, Ellington had a quick glimpse of his face. He had only seen photos of Campbell, but the guy sure looked a lot like him. Ellington dashed quickly back to his hiding place and watched as the man strode to his car.

Ellington raced down the driveway and upon reaching the street was just in time to see the Mercedes turn right at the end. Again, darkness was Ellington's friend and he took advantage of it by staying relatively close and keeping his prey well in sight. He again called Bellamy. 'I think I might be following Campbell.'

'If that's the case, you *do* need backup. Where are you now?'

Ellington checked his navigator. 'I'm on Pennant Hills Road, just passed Blackwood Street. He's got his indicator on. He's going to turn left.'

'I'll contact the local guys,' Bellamy said.

'Hang on, he's turned again. We're now in Nancy Street and he's pulled into the kerb. He's stopped at the old brick quarry.' Ellington pulled into the kerb near the corner and watched as the man left his car and started down the timber steps leading into the quarry. 'He's going down into the quarry.'

'Okay, keep out of his way 'till the local guys get there.'

Ellington walked towards the staircase. He passed a huge sign warning the public against entering and threatening heavy fines. Ellington, like most Sydneysiders, had heard about the quarry and the contention and squabbling that surrounded it. The most recent news was that it had been sold to developers who were planning to build a multi-storey apartment block.

Ellington watched as the man clambered down the staircase into the bowels of the quarry. He waited until the stairway was clear before following down. A freezing wind had sprung up, and it swirled around him as he descended. Away from the street lights, the darkness was so intense he couldn't see his hand before him. He stumbled forward on uneven rocky ground cursing that he hadn't thought to bring a torch. He was relying on the pale glow from the man's torch as it lit up the path ahead Trees had grown during the many years of the quarry's disuse, and Ellington felt their sharp sting as branches brushed his face. After several minutes the torch lit up the quarry wall. They had travelled the quarry's full width. Ellington stopped and watched. The torch was moving again lighting up an area that appeared to be a shallow grotto carved by nature into the quarry's wall. The man was on his knees pulling at branches lying on the ground. The torch was now on a rocky ledge above, and even in its diffused light, Ellington could see the stark white shape that was being uncovered. The girl's body was a mass of wounds. Blood was caked from her head to her feet and two big patches on her face filled Ellington with horror. He froze as he saw the man withdraw a huge hunting knife from his coat pocket. Ellington pulled out his firearm and yelled. 'Drop the knife, I've got you covered.' The man turned, a look of surprise and alarm contorting his features. He stood slowly, hands in the air but still holding the knife. In a lightning move he flipped the torch from the ledge, plunging the area into total darkness. Ellington heard the crunch of leaves and a heavy footstep. Then came the swish of metal as the knife narrowly missed him. He took a step back, but then another swish and he felt cold steel cutting across his upper arm and shoulder. He could hear the man's heavy breathing and without aim, fired his gun. A guttural grunt followed by a thud told him he had found his mark. Silence followed. Ellington searched briefly for the torch but unable to find it, clumsily made his way in the darkness back to the staircase. As he drew near, he heard the screech of police sirens. The streetlight illuminated the staircase and the six police officers descending it. They all wore protective vests and helmets. Their strong torches flooded him in light.

'DS Ellington, South Sydney,' he muttered. He realised he still had his pistol in his hand. He shoved it in his pocket and fumbled for his ID. 'Suspect down, took a bullet, don't know his condition, but he's dangerous, has a weapon. There's a body there too.'

'Sergeant, you have been wounded. I'll call the ambos. Wait here 'till they come…okay?'

Ellington nodded and looked down at his left hand which was gathering copious amounts of blood. He slowly climbed the stairs and sat at the top watching the torchlight flitting around the quarry. His breath formed puffs of steam as it mingled with the cold air. His arm was now throbbing and he had an overpowering desire to lie down and sleep. He was losing focus on the quarry when an ambulance screeched into the street. He remembered being helped into the ambulance and then the blackness came.

*

He awoke in a warm bed. A blinding light filled his senses and for a split second, he wondered if he might be in heaven. He moved a little but found himself restricted on both sides by tubes. A soft hand lifted his, and he looked into the face of an angel. He found out seconds later it was not an angel but Nurse Emma O'Gorman. She pressed her fingers against his wrist and looked at the little watch hanging from a ribbon around her neck. Satisfied, she gently dropped his hand, looked at him and smiled. 'Welcome back.'

'Did I lose my arm?' he asked.

'Not at all. Your big jacket helped miles. It's all stained and bloody, but you should keep it as a good luck talisman.' Her accent was soft, lilting Irish. 'But you've got a bounty lot of stitches there. You have a serious wound and you've lost a lot of blood.'

'What's all this?' Ellington glared at the jangle of tubes.

'Intravenous antibiotics and all sorts of other goodies to help you with the pain and all.'

'Did they catch Campbell?"

'To be sure. He's in this very hospital.'

Ellington gasped. Emma saw the look on his face and laughed. 'Two floors up and with feet cuffed to the bed.'

'So, I didn't kill him,' he said wistfully.

'No. He'll live to face the music. You got him in the abdomen, no vital organs, but he'll suffer.'

'When can I get out of here?'

'When the doctor says you can.'

Tony Salerno arrived that afternoon with a bag containing a shirt, underwear and a toothbrush.

Ellington smiled. 'Thanks Sal. Whose gear is this?'

'Mine. The toothbrush's new.'

'Pleased to know that. Thanks mate. They're not letting me out of here 'till tomorrow. Did anyone pick up my car?'

'Me and Pascoe picked it up a little while ago. Pascoe drove it back to the station.' Salerno looked around the room. 'This hospital's not far from the murder scene.'

'Campbell's here too.'

'I know.' Salerno sat by the bed. 'You did a great job, Duke. Everyone's calling you a hero.'

'Rubbish.' Ellington tried to prop himself up but the

31

jangle of tubes defeated him. 'Have they identified the girl?' he asked.

'Yeah, the one reported missing...Teagan Rogers. There's also evidence that Campbell killed that other girl...the one we found in the warehouse, Melanie Churchill.'

'I know. Campbell's blood was found on the window sill of the warehouse storeroom. It seems Campbell was still meddling with the body when Ed Duncan arrived. Campbell probably heard Duncan outside getting the key. and made his escape through the window.'

'A can of petrol was found not far from the body and it looks pretty definite Campbell planned to burn it and destroy his DNA. There was a can of petrol in the quarry near Teagan's body too. Again, he was interrupted...this time by you. Bellamy's been in touch with the Queensland police. He thinks those two murders up there were Campbell's work...the time frame, the burning, the mutilations.'

*

Ellington's body returned to normal but his mind didn't. The months leading up to Campbell's trial were filled with turmoil and terrifying nightmares. He thought the trial would release him, and bring closure. But it didn't. He gave his evidence and heard the stifled gasps of horror as the jury listened to the lurid details of the defendant's abhorrent crimes. He watched Campbell sitting in the dock with a faraway stare in his pale icy eyes, a loose smile playing around the thick lips, and his chubby almost grand-daddy face calm and composed.

Campbell's lawyer did his best but couldn't compete with the overwhelming evidence which came mainly from Ellington and Ivana Mirrakoff. The female judge, obviously moved by the horrific revelations, imposed the maximum sentence, life without parole. The sentence was no sooner out of the judge's mouth when Campbell turned his huge strong body, pointed a finger at Ellington and drew it across his throat. He then poked out his tongue and wiggled it from side to side.

CHAPTER 3
November 2021

Ellington shudders as he recalls the scene in court. He knows Campbell is locked away, so why the nightmares, these manifestations of terror which after all this time, are still crippling him emotionally and leaving him fearful, dejected and depressed?

He looks sideways at Sarah. She turns and meets his gaze. 'Where are we going Sarge?'

'Summer Hill…nearly there.' He makes a left-hand turn leaving behind the heavy traffic and suffocating fumes of Parramatta Road. When his navigator states: *you have reached your destination*, he pulls into the kerb and surveys his surroundings. Summer Hill is an old suburb some ten kilometres south of the city. Sarah sits uncomfortably, pulling at the cuticle on her thumb nail, a bad habit that materialises every time she feels tense. They had travelled thirty minutes, and Ellington hadn't uttered a word since the four he spoke ten minutes earlier.

Their destination Hamilton Street is long and narrow. The houses lining both sides are a mixture of Californian bungalows and Federation cottages. A few Victorian mansions in various states of repair are sprinkled haphazardly on the high side of the road. Some of these have been lovingly restored to their former grandeur. The house they have come to is such a house, a well-maintained Victorian, painted white with touches of blue. A lacy wrought iron balustrade guards a narrow balcony on the upper level. A painted concrete path lined both sides with tall rose bushes, leads to the front porch.

'I love roses', Sarah sniffs.

Ellington strides on without comment. There are no bells or buttons, only a brass knocker. Ellington knocks three times before the door is opened by a man with hang-dog eyes set into a pale craggy face.

'Detective Sergeant Ellington and Senior Constable Bradley,' They show their IDs.

'David Seymour, come in.' Seymour opens the door and stands back while they enter. They follow him through a short vestibule leading into a dimly lit room. Green velvet lounge chairs match the closed drapes which conceal the long narrow windows. A patterned green carpet does nothing to lift the dreary decor. The room has the faint musty smell of one rarely used. A woman with shoulder-length fair hair sits in a semi-reclining position on the lounge. Her eyes are watery, red-rimmed and puffy. Ellington estimates the woman to be in her mid-forties.

'This is my wife, Janet. Please sit.' Seymour indicates the two opposite chairs and sits next to his wife. Ellington takes out his notebook. Long ago he decided he preferred the old fashion way. The others could use their battery-fed recorders, but he prefers to put it all down by hand. It helps him remember. Before speaking he looks at the woman who is fidgeting with her handkerchief, working it in all directions. She seems utterly traumatised. Ellington clears his throat and speaks.

'You reported your daughter missing at two this morning. Correct?'

'Yes. Janet wanted to call earlier, but I didn't want us

to sound like alarmists.'

'When was the last time you saw your daughter?'

'Sunday afternoon.'

'That the last time?'

'I'm a politician. I live half my life in Canberra.'

'How was she on Sunday?'

'We went to church. She was in her comfort zone there, happy enough, I think.' His eyes squint in thought.

'Did she say anything that was at all unusual?'

Seymour gives a slight shrug and crimps his lips tightly. 'Not that I remember.'

'What about the last few weeks? Was there anything unusual in her manner?'

'As you can imagine, when Parliament is sitting, I don't see much of my family, only weekends. I usually drive back to Canberra Sunday afternoon.'

Ellington shifts his gaze to Janet Seymour. 'Do you remember Elise saying anything that might indicate things might not be normal?'

Janet shakes her head slowly.

'When was the last time *you* saw your daughter?'

'I saw her yesterday morning, before she left for work.' Janet's voice is brittle.

'How was she?'

'Her usual quiet self.'

'Nothing to indicate she was planning to go off somewhere?'

'No.'

'You said she was leaving for work. Where is this?'

'The local chemist.'

'Where exactly is the chemist?'

'Station Street, near the railway. The chemist's name is Nathan Brown.'

'When did you expect her home?'

'Usually around six thirty, the shop closes at six. Elise helps to close up and then walks home.'

Ellington scribbles in his notebook. Without looking up he asks, 'your daughter's date of birth please.'

'Sixth November nineteen ninety-eight.'

'So, she's recently turned twenty-three,' Ellington mumbles to himself. He looks up and speaks directly to Janet.

'Tell me exactly what happened from the moment you got up yesterday morning to when your daughter left the house.'

Janet's mouth contorts as she tries to control her emotions. She takes a deep breath and speaks shakily: 'Well, I got up at the usual time, seven, went down to the kitchen, put the kettle on for tea, and then on to Elise's room. I knocked and called for her to get up.' The woman gulps and her eyes seem to roll. For a minute Ellington thinks she's going to faint. Janet slowly regains her composure. 'Elise came to the table and had her toast and tea. She didn't say anything, but then again, she never chatted much at breakfast. She went back to her bedroom.' The woman's voice trails off and she stares into her lap.

'And?' Ellington prompts.

'Around eight she said goodbye and left. I waved her off at the door.'

'Did you see what direction she took?'

'Yes, the usual one, down towards Douglas Street.'

'There was nothing at all about her manner or appearance that could lead you to believe Elise was planning to go away?'

'Not at all,' Janet's eyes fasten on her husband and then back to Ellington. 'I think she's been abducted.'

'Why do you think that?'

'What else could have happened? She wouldn't just go off somewhere without telling us, and if she'd had an accident, we'd know by now.'

'What was she wearing?'

'Her red dress, she looked lovely.'

'Can you describe the dress?'

'I made that dress. I make all her clothes. I think I might still have the pattern with a photo.'

'Perhaps you could find it when we're finished here. What sort of shoes was she wearing?'

'Black courts.'

'Courts?'

'Court shoes, like the ones I'm wearing.' Janet pushes forward her left foot showing a plain black shoe. 'Only Elise's shoes had a higher heel.'

'Did she take a bag or anything?'

'She had her handbag, the one she always takes to work.'

'Have you checked to see what's missing from her room?'

'Yes, her mobile phone, her wallet and some makeup.'

'Have you tried phoning the mobile?'

'Of course,' David Seymour growls. 'It's turned off.'

'What would be in her wallet?'

'Her credit card, her driver's licence, some cash. I'm not sure what else.'

'I'll need to know her banking and credit card details.'

'No problem, we have the numbers in our filing system.'

'When did you arrive back from Canberra sir?'

'Around two this morning. When Janet phoned last night, she sounded quite distressed. I thought it necessary to get home.'

'So yesterday, you were sitting in Parliament?'

'Correct.'

'It's important that I establish the whereabouts of all involved persons.' Ellington turns his attention to Janet who is dabbing her eyes. 'How did *you* spend yesterday, Mrs Seymour?' There is a long silence before Janet speaks.

'I was at home all day, sewing. I did a little gardening.'

'Could Elise be with a friend?'

'Elise didn't have any friends.' David scowls.

'No friends? Are you new to the area?'

'We've been here twenty years.'

'Then how come Elise doesn't have friends?'

'She *did* have friends, but not after the engagement broke up.'

'Engagement?'

The Seymours exchange glances. Janet's expression changes from grief to anger. 'Elise was engaged to a boy, Richard Ballantyne. They went together for three years. She met him at tennis soon after she finished school.'

'He was her first and only boyfriend,' David mutters.

'He had a few friends and they became Elise's friends,' Janet adds.

'I'll need their names.'

'She hasn't mixed with any of them for nearly a year.'

'Just the same, I'll need their names.'

'There was Tara Gresham. She was going out with Travis'... Janet wrinkles her brow. 'I can't remember his last name, can you David?'

David shakes his head.

Janet continues. 'Travis and Richard were apparently best mates. There was another couple. They came here a few times. The girl's name was Courtney, but for the life of me, I can't remember the fellow's name.'

'It was a funny name,' cuts in David.

Ellington scribbles and looks up. 'Go on,' he prompts.

'Well, when Elise turned twenty, she and Richard became engaged. We didn't really approve of Richard. He didn't have much of a job, he was in real estate. I always thought he was a bit conceited.' David pauses and looks to Janet for support.

'Yes, I agree, he was very conceited.' Janet's head sinks to her chest. She breathes a heavy sigh.

Ellington breaks the silence. 'Go on please.'

'Elise and Tara became close friends. I didn't approve of her either. I thought she was common,' Janet murmurs.

Ellington narrows his eyes. What a funny word, a word his grandmother might have used.

'Well, everything was going'... Seymour pauses and cocks his head to one side, 'okay, until about a year ago. Out of the blue, Richard broke off the engagement and the next thing we know, he's moved in with Tara Gresham. Elise's heart was broken. She had lost her fiancé and her best friend in the one go.'

Janet's lips tighten into a thin line. 'They were a pair of traitors.'

'And then?'

Janet sobs quietly. 'I can't handle this.'

'Elise threw in her law degree and resigned from her job.' David's tone is bitter.

'She was studying law?'

'She was articled to the firm she was working with.'

'Why did she throw in her degree, her job?'

'Tara worked for the same firm. Elise couldn't bear to be near the girl.' David's eyes flit around the room before settling on a large old-fashioned oil painting on the opposite wall. 'We tried to talk her out of it...letting those two worthless creatures wreck her career.'

'But she did it anyway,' Janet says sadly.

'And Tara is still with the firm?'

'Yes, but the irony is, she only got the job because of Elise. She'd been unemployed for months. Elise put in a good word for her.' David's mirthless smile doesn't reach his eyes.

'Tara was doing law too?'

'No, she was just a clerk. When Elise told us she was resigning, I contacted Tara and begged her to leave, so Elise could continue with her degree, but the bitch wouldn't budge. She said she didn't mind working in the same place as Elise, and if Elise couldn't handle it, then it was up to her to leave.' Janet sniffs into her handkerchief.

'Has Elise seen any of these people since the breakup?'

'She sees Richard every day. He passes the shop on his way to the train. There's no contact,' Janet whispers.

'What about the other couple?' Ellington glances at his notes. 'Courtney?'

'She phoned several times, but Elise wouldn't talk to her. She thought everyone was conspiring against her.'

'Did Elise try to get articled to another law firm?'

'No. We suggested it, but she'd lost all interest.'

'Siblings?'

'Elise was our only child,' David offers sadly.

There's a short silence as Ellington scribbles. He looks up and asks: 'When did Elise start working for the chemist?'

'About nine months ago. After she left the law firm, she just sat around moping for three months. Then out of the blue she announced that the local chemist had advertised for an assistant, and she was applying for the job.'

Ellington scribbles again then looks directly at Janet. 'When Elise failed to come home last night, what exactly did you do?'

'By seven thirty I was starting to get a bit edgy. Thursday is one of the nights Elise always eats with us. She's never late on Thursdays. It was when I went to phone her mobile that I found our phone off the hook.'

'Off the hook?'

'Yes, we have a handset phone in the study.'

'How long had the phone been off the hook?'

'I don't know, possibly all day. I could have knocked it, or maybe not hung up properly. It was only *just* off the hook. It was no use calling the pharmacy, they close at six. I don't know the chemist's private number, I don't even know where he lives, and with a name like Brown, I'd never pick it from the directory. Then it occurred to me that Elise had probably been trying to contact me and couldn't get through with the phone being off the hook. But when it came ten o'clock, I phoned David. He said he would drive home straight away, and suggested I contact Pastor Allenby.'

Ellington's eyebrows shoot up in question. David responds wearily. 'He's our local pastor. Elise had helped him with his accounts a couple of times over the past six months or so. I thought maybe he had asked her to call around after work. He was the only person I could think of.'

'So, what did Pastor Allenby have to say?'

'He hadn't seen or heard from Elise since last Sunday.'

'What happened last Sunday?'

'Church of course,' Janet Seymour mutters. 'The three of us go every Sunday.'

'And Elise has no friends there?'

'Elise is the only young person in the congregation, most are our vintage. Some are considerably older.'

'Elise goes every Sunday?'

'It's the highlight of her week. She's a very religious girl.

She loves the people and they all love her, she's an inspiration to them.   She works tirelessly for the church.'

'Which church are we talking about?'

'It's in Apple Street. You wouldn't know it's a church, we're not allowed to put up a sign, we're not a formally recognised church,' Janet sighs.

'Our church is called: The Church of Jesus and his Saints,' David prompts.

'It's connected to the Mormon Church then?'

'No nothing to do with the Mormon Church. It's our church. It's on its own, not connected to anything.' Janet says defensively.

'Maybe we should tell you a bit about our church,' David offers. 'For years Janet and I attended the local Anglican church. A new minister came about three years ago. He started preaching all sorts of stuff that most of us didn't believe in. He was all for gay marriage, said cannabis was okay for medical purposes, was totally in favour of euthanasia, all the things most of us thought were sinful. Some of the congregation started complaining to each other. I heard grumbles at golf, Janet heard them at croquet, and it wasn't long before we realised there was quite a contingent of people very upset.   A delegation of us approached him, but he refused to change his tone. We complained to the bishop, but that didn't do any good either. And then my sister who lives in Dunkley, happened to mention that their local minister had been.... removed from the church because he was wrongfully accused of something or another. According to my sister, he was a remarkable man, full of goodness and compassion. Now his career was ended all because of spiteful gossip. This gave us an idea. We called together all those who had expressed dissatisfaction with the current situation and had a meeting. Nearly fifty people turned up. It was agreed we form a breakaway church, and if the Dunkley pastor was available, invite him to be our minister. Our numbers grew when word got out. One of the people had a house in Apple Street he wanted to rent out. Each family pledged a weekly sum to pay the rent and provide a modest salary for Pastor Allenby. We also had to foot the costs of converting the house into a church. Many of us provided free labour. We knocked down walls and turned four rooms into one. We left the kitchen, bathroom, a bedroom and a small sitting room for Pastor Allenby's living quarters.'

'And when did Elise become involved?'

'Around the same time Richard dumped her. Our new church came at the right time for her. It gave her comfort,' David says sadly.

'She wasn't a devoted church goer prior?'

David clears his throat. 'No. Those people she mixed with weren't exactly church going types. It was only after she left them, she turned to the church.'

Janet breaks in: 'Everyone loves Elise, she's their little angel. She's so different from other young ones around today. Some people think Elise has saintly qualities. She's always being held up as an example of goodness and compassion. We're so proud of her. Pastor Allenby often has her read the Lessons at service, and once when he had a bad throat, she actually read his sermon.'

'Elise gives up her Saturday afternoons to take two ladies shopping and Tuesday and Friday nights she cooks dinner for a very debilitated elderly parishioner,' David states proudly.

Ellington frowning looks up from his notebook. 'Social media, Facebook, Twitter?'

'Elise is not involved in any of that. She doesn't have a computer.'

'That's a bit unusual, isn't it?'

'She had an iPad, and was involved in all that stuff when she was going with Ballantyne, but after the break up, she gave it away.'

'Where's the iPad?'

'She gave it to the girl at the chemist.'

'Just gave it away?'

'She said she had no further use for it.'

Ellington takes a deep breath. 'You had better give me a list of people Elise visits and their addresses, and of course we will need to talk with Mr Allenby.' Ellington stands. 'When you phoned the chemist shop this morning, who did you speak to?'

'Nathan Brown, the owner.'

'And?'

'I asked him if he knew where Elise was. He said when Elise hadn't turned up by nine-thirty yesterday morning he tried her mobile first, and then us. Of course, he didn't get through, the phone being off the hook. When we learned that Elise hadn't been at the shop at all yesterday, we were utterly distraught.'

'So, no one in the chemist shop or anywhere else, as far as you know, saw Elise after she left here yesterday morning?'

'As far as we know,' Janet murmurs.

'So, when Elise left here yesterday, she walked down Hamilton Street, and then?'

'About fifty metres up she would cross the road and walk down Douglas Street. That road takes her to Station Street and the shopping centre.'

'It appears that after Elise left here around eight yesterday, something happened between here and the chemist shop.' Ellington looks from one face to the other.

'Would Elise be in the habit of talking with anyone, say a neighbour, on her walk to work?'

'If she did, she never mentioned it. Although we've been here twenty years, we don't know many neighbours, just the people directly opposite and the ones next door, and of course the church people,' David says.

'Does Elise pass any of the church people's houses on her way to work?'

'Most live nearby, but Elise doesn't actually walk past any of their houses on her way to work.'

'Is it possible that she might have accepted a lift? Someone who offered her a ride to work and then...?'

'That's possible, but I don't know who. Elise wouldn't get into a car unless she knew the driver,' says Janet.

'Do you have a photo of your daughter?'

Without answering, Janet turns to the small table beside her. She slides open the single drawer, withdraws a silver framed photograph, and hands it to Ellington. The young woman looking at him with a quirky almost contemptuous expression is not what he had expected. This is not the angelic vision described by the Seymours. The girl sits astride a huge motorbike. Her jet-black hair is short and spiky, and she wears a nose ring. Her plunging black singlet top, fails to cover the colourful tattoo on her shoulder.

'Is this recent?'

'No. That was taken probably two years ago.'

'Why do you keep this picture in a drawer?'

'Elise hates it. She gets upset if she sees it.'

'Why?'

'It reminds her of her other life.'

'How tall is Elise?'

'Five nine.'

'Tall', he murmurs.

'We're a tall family.'

'Did Elise have any enemies?'

'Of course not,' says David.

'Do you or Mrs Seymour have enemies?'

'Politicians are often in situations where they might not always be particularly popular, but enemies? No.'

'What about that lobbyist, David?' Janet asks.

'Partridge? He's harmless.'

'He didn't sound harmless when he threatened you.'

'Tell me.' Ellington stares hard at David.

'A few weeks ago, Stuart Partridge made an appointment to see me. We discussed a Bill the Government is planning to introduce into Parliament. The Bill has the support of the Government apart from two members. The Opposition is completely opposed to it, and we three Independents hold the balance. Partridge works for the Government and he's been hounding the three of us non-stop. It's possible he might have won over one of the others, but Adam Jenkins and I are holding out. The more I consider it, the more I'm certain I'll oppose it. I don't believe the State police should be compromised by the Feds.'

'The State Police?'

'Yes. It will take away their powers in certain areas. I'm afraid I can't say any more than that.'

'Tell me about your meeting with this Partridge.'

'He started off all smarmy and pleasant. I was non-committal and didn't say much. Then he started applying pressure. I said I would not be told what to do and that I had made up my mind to oppose the Bill. He was furious and said if I didn't toe the line, I'd be sorry, or words to that effect.'

'And?'

'I told him to get out.'

'Have you seen or heard from him since?'

'No.'

'I might have to speak with him. Have you an address?'

'Yes, he's in Canberra. I'll get it for you.' Ellington turns to Janet. 'We'll need to see Elise's room. While we're at it, could you find the photo of the dress she was wearing yesterday? I'll need the number and password of her bank account too.'

Janet nods and awkwardly pulls herself to her feet. She stands rigidly for a few seconds and then starts to sway. Sarah rushes towards her, offering a steadying hand.

'Are you alright Mrs Seymour? '

She straightens and smiles wanly. 'I'm alright. I'll get what you want.'

David returns and hands Ellington a note. 'That's Partridge's home address.'

'Could we see Elise's room please?'

'It's the room at the end of the hall, come this way.' They follow David down the short hallway. He pauses outside a closed door. 'You can go in. It's unlocked.'

Entering the room Ellington is hit with the strong combined aroma of lavender, lilac and roses. Sarah follows, sniffing. The room is large for a bedroom. Its main feature is the double bed, an ornate affair covered in a quilted pink satin spread. A sheer pink organza canopy falls from a bronze frame. Bunches of potpourri sachets hang from the bedposts, and pink and lilac satin pillows are piled on the top end. A mobile of coloured glass angels hangs above the bed moving slowly to the rhythm of the soft breeze which floats through the lacy pink curtains. An old-fashioned dressing table and matching chair swathed in pink satin, stand beside the window. Decorative perfume bottles and a silver hairbrush are displayed on the dressing table. An antique wardrobe stands next to the doorway alongside a small cupboard. A row of bookshelves and a television occupy one wall, and a large framed Monet print decorates another. The carpet is pink plush.

'Wow,' Sarah squeaks. 'It's like something out of Grimm's Fairy Tales.'

'This girl is something of an anomaly. That photo they showed us...she looks like a biker's moll, and then we hear she's an angel in disguise, loved for her saintly deeds...and now this room.'

Sarah shakes her head wistfully. 'It's weird, just look at that bed!'

'I'll look through the dressing table, and you go through those books. Be thorough, make sure there's nothing hidden.'

Sarah moves to the bookshelf and picks up a book. Ellington turns his attention to the dressing table. He sits on the chair and examines the perfume bottles. He opens each one and sniffs. All are as they appear, just perfume. The first drawer contains a neat pile of handkerchiefs and an assortment of boxes. Each small box contains an item of jewellery, either a ring or earrings. Ellington knows enough about jewellery to decide nothing looks particularly valuable. The larger boxes contain necklaces and bracelets, all colour coordinated. The second drawer contains makeup and multiple face creams all neatly boxed. The third drawer contains eye drops and several bottles of pills. These take Ellington's close attention. Most of the pills are labelled vitamins...one is a prescribed medication, Prozac. Why is Elise taking Prozac? Ellington pulls a plastic bag from his briefcase and drops all the bottles in. Even those that appear to be vitamins will be tested. He pulls open the bottom drawer and finds two pairs of sunglasses, a camera, an address book and a photograph album. He flicks through the address book and drops it into his plastic bag. He then checks the camera for photos. All appear to have been erased. But the album is another matter. He opens it and is hit with a full-page photograph of a beautiful young woman. The girl smiling for the camera is tall and slim with blonde hair falling in loose curls. She wears a knee-length white dress splashed with red roses. As he stares at the photo, Ellington is transported back in time to another album, his grandmother's. As a teenager she wore clothes like this...beautiful, feminine dresses from the fifties. He is staring at the photo when Sarah yells. 'Hey, I found her diary.' She triumphantly throws the diary onto the dressing table and at the same time sees the photo Ellington is studying. 'Who is *that?*'

'I don't know but she looks a bit like Marilyn Monroe.'

'Who is Marilyn Monroe?'

'A movie star from the fifties, I can't believe you don't know.'

'What's *she* doing in this album?'

'It's not Marilyn Monroe,' mutters Ellington. He takes another look. The girl in the photo does seem somehow familiar He turns the page and there she is again in yet another lovely old-fashioned dress, this time with a man.

'That's David Seymour,' squeaks Sarah.

Ellington peers closely at the girl's face. After a few seconds, his eyes widen. 'That's Elise Seymour!'

'What she doing dressed up like that?'

'We need to have another talk with the parents.'

Ellington picks up the diary and flips through the pages. Some of the pages are covered in small neat handwriting. Others are covered in numbers and symbols. The last entry is coded and dated Wednesday the fourteenth of November, the day before she disappeared. He drops it into his plastic bag along with the album.

'Nothing else in the books?'

'No. She had a lot of books I've never heard of.'

Ellington opens the wardrobe and the smell of lavender is pleasantly overpowering. Hanging from coat hangers in a neat row is a number of beautiful frocks. It's an astounding collection belonging to a long past decade.

'Wow. Look at this!' Sarah pulls one out on its hanger and swirls it around, a sheer lilac creation flocked with tiny white flowers. She puts it back, and pulls out another. 'And this!' the dress is deep pink with a full silky skirt falling from a small fitted waist. Sarah holds it up against her body, and peers in the mirror. 'Pretty, but I wouldn't be seen dead in any of them,' she huffs, hanging the dress back.

'What do you wear when you're not in uniform Constable?' Ellington grins, as he pulls open the top drawer of the wardrobe.

'When I meet my mates at the pub, I wear my jeans and a tee.'

'What if you were going somewhere special?'

'I'd wear my jeans and a fancy tee.'

'What if it was too cold for a tee?'

'I'd take my leather jacket.' Sarah smiles and thinks: *Sergeant Ellington is a flesh and blood person after all.* She can feel herself starting to relax.

Ellington picks up a stack of neatly piled underwear and runs his hand along the back of the drawer. The second drawer contains sheer pantyhose and a small pile of socks and gloves. Folded knitwear takes up the third and fourth drawers and a pile of fragrant nightgowns are in the fifth. He makes a clumsy attempt to tidy up the delicate garments.

'I wouldn't worry Sarge, I don't think she'll be back.'

'Why is that?' he asks closing the drawer.

'Don't know, just got a feeling.'

'What's on top of that cupboard?'

'Looks like a thingamy to play music.'

Ellington examines the old-fashioned record player.

It's a turntable,' He opens the cupboard door and pulls out a small stack of records. 'And this is what you play.' He picks up the top record and reads: *The Best of Nat King Cole.'*

'Who is Nat King Cole?'

'Nat King Cole was a singer in the fifties, very good and very popular.'

'How come you know all this fifties stuff?'

Ellington chuckles and picks up another record. 'Perry Como. I think our Elise has entered a time warp. I wonder why.'

'Something to do with her broken engagement?'

'Possibly, the photo Janet Seymour presented showed a very different person to the one we see here. Let's have another chat with her.' Ellington replaces the records and closes the cupboard door.

The Seymours are still sitting in the lounge room. 'I have some items here that I need to borrow. I'll write you a receipt. I can assure you they will be returned.'

'What are they?' David asks.

Ellington empties the contents onto the sofa. 'When did Elise start taking Prozac and why was she taking it?'

Janet fidgets with her handkerchief before speaking. 'Elise went through a very traumatic time twelve months ago when Richard dumped her. She was severely depressed. I took her to the local doctor and he prescribed Prozac. She's been on it ever since.'

'Was she formally diagnosed?'

'Yes. She's bipolar. That's why I know she hasn't just run off. She wouldn't have left those tablets behind. She relies on them.'

Ellington nods and opens the album displaying the first

photo. 'When was this photo taken?'

Janet looks mournfully at the photo. 'That was taken a few months ago, I think.'

'Why did you show us the photo of Elise on the bike if this is more recent? She looks vastly different here.' Ellington stabs the photo with a finger.

'I'd forgotten about those. That's how Elise looked before and after Rick, and the other one I showed you, was how she looked when she was with Rick.'

Ellington raises his eyebrows. 'Well, these are the photos we'll be using in our investigation.'

Janet nods, 'of course.'

'Why did Elise change her appearance?'

'Do you mean when she cut and coloured her hair and had herself tattooed?'

'Yes.'

'To fit in with Ballantyne and his crowd,' Janet sighs. 'She acted tough, brash, just to fit in.'

'And then she changed her appearance back again when she left that group. She also changed back as a person, softer, caring, refined,' David adds.

'The Elise in those photos is the real Elise.' Janet points at the album.

'Would you mind looking at the names in this address book and telling me if Elise had been in recent contact with any of these people.' He hands the book to Janet. Her forehead creases into three horizontal lines as she reads.

'She had regular contact with all these people, she sees them at church. Two of them are the ladies she takes shopping, Esther and Joan. Maude Tingwell is the lady she visits on Tuesday and Friday nights.'

'Does Elise have a car?'

'She had one, but she sold it.'

'How does she take elderly ladies shopping without a car?'

'She borrows mine.'

'And this happens every Saturday?'

'Yes, most Saturday afternoons. She works at the shop in the morning.'

'And the lady she visits in the evening, she drives to her?'

'No, Mrs Tingwell lives close to the shop. Elise goes straight from work, she walks.'

'And the parson?'

'The church is nearby too. We go there by car on Sundays, but on the couple of occasions Elise called in to help Pastor Allenby, she would have walked.'

'I'll need to talk to Pastor Allenby and all those church goers.' Ellington puts out his hand and Janet limply gives him the address book. 'What time are your Sunday services?'

'There's only the one service. It starts at nine-thirty and finishes around eleven. We stay on for an hour or so having morning tea and a chat.'

Ellington raises his eyebrows in thought. 'It could be a good opportunity for me to talk to them all. I'll turn up for the morning tea.'

Seymour wrinkles his brow. 'Detective, these people are very private. I think it would cause them great discomfort to be answering questions in public. It would be much better if you interviewed them in their homes.'

'Oh, I won't be interviewing anyone…just a few simple questions.' Ellington sits on the sofa beside the spilled items. There is an uncomfortable silence as he records each one in his notebook before returning it to the bag. He tears the page from the book and hands it to David. 'That's a list of all the items I'm taking. Did you manage to find a photo of the dress

Elise was wearing?' Janet picks up a package from beside her and hands it to him. The model on the cover is tall and slim. The dress is in the same mode as the ones in Elise's room, fifties vintage. The small piece of material pinned to the pattern is a finely woven fabric in bright red. 'This is the material you used?'

'Yes.'

'Stunning. Your daughter would be quite noticeable in this outfit, a tall attractive blonde.'

'She is very attractive,' Seymour mutters.

'Have you got her bank details?'

Seymour hands him a slip of note paper. 'She only had one account.'

'I'll start a door knock and see if any of the neighbours saw anything. I really will need to talk with Richard Ballantyne and his girlfriend. Can you tell me how I can contact them?'

'Ballantyne worked for an estate agent in Croydon. He may be still with them. Tara works at Melville and Son in the city. I think she and Ballantyne live in Stewart Street, not far from here.'

Ellington scribbles in his book and walks to the door. 'Thank you. I'll see you on Sunday. If something significant occurs, please phone me.' He fishes in his wallet and hands David Seymour his card.

CHAPTER 4

In the short time they were in the house, the sky has clouded over and a cool wind has developed.

'Okay Constable, you knock that side and I'll do this. Cross over to Douglas Street and I'll meet you at the end. Take notes as you go, make sure you get everyone's name, etcetera. Here, take this.' He carefully extracts one of the photos from the album.

Only five people in Hamilton Street open their doors to Sarah. Not one had seen Elise on Thursday morning nor had anything unusual to report. Ellington's experience is the same. He is about to turn away from the last house before crossing to Douglas Street when the front door swings open. An elderly man squints at him through wizened eyes. 'Yeah?'

Ellington flashes his identification. 'Detective Sergeant Ellington. I'm investigating the disappearance of a young woman who was last seen on her way down this street early yesterday morning.' He holds open the album. 'Have you seen this girl in the last twenty-four hours?' The man peers at the photo and rubs his stubbly chin.

'No. I think I saw her passing by a week or so ago, but not in the last few days.'

'Anything unusual happen around here yesterday sir?'

'No, but I found a mobile phone in the gutter this

morning.'

Ellington's eyes widen at the unexpected news. 'Could I see it sir?'

The man nods and shuffles off. As he waits, Ellington absently watches a small beetle struggling in a spider's web. He flicks it free with his hand and nods with satisfaction as it crawls away. The man returns and hands him a nondescript mobile phone. 'I looked in it to see if I could find a name or somethin'. I wanted to get it back to its owner. I don't know much about those things, never 'ad one meself.' Ellington flips the mobile open and goes to *contacts*. The first name is *Gregory Allenby*.

'What time did you find this?'

'When I went out to get me newspaper, that's when I saw it in the gutter. It would 'ave been around seven o'clock.'

'Thank you. We may need to talk to you again. Could I have your name please?'

'Woodley, Alf Woodley.'

'And a contact number?'

On the footpath, Ellington flicks through the phone and looks at calls. A message causes his eyes to narrow and his lips to compress.

Hamilton Street forms a T intersection with Dixon Street at its north end. Douglas Street runs at right angles midway across Hamilton. Both Dixon and Douglas streets run into Station Street. Ellington meets Sarah at the shopping centre. Together they have spoken with only ten residents.

Small shops of various kinds line both sides of Station Street. Some have tried to lighten the dreary area by erecting colourful awnings. At the railway end of the street, an ancient hotel stands opposite a supermarket.

'Any luck?' Sarah asks.

'I found her mobile.'

'Where was it?'

'In the gutter at the end of Hamilton Street.'

'Anything useful?'

'Yes, a very interesting message.'

'Well?'

'Let's talk first with the chemist.' Ellington strides towards the pharmacy.

The pleasant smell of perfume mingles with faint chemical odours. A counter with a cash register stands near the door. Shelving loaded with everything from face creams to cough syrup occupies three walls. A few small square tables have been set up in the middle of the room, displaying perfumes, cosmetics and baby products. Located at the far end of the room is a counter. Above it, hangs a curved board with the word *Prescriptions* displayed in large letters.

'Can I help you?' A young woman suddenly appears from behind one of the tables. She wears a pharmacy coat that stretches tightly around her generous frame. Her dark hair is streaked with blonde and billows down to her shoulders in loose curls. She surveys them through small, dark, intense eyes.

Ellington and Sarah show their IDs. 'Detective Sergeant Ellington and Senior Constable Bradley. We're investigating the disappearance of Elise Seymour.' The girl's face clouds and her mouth tightens. 'Haven't you found her?'

'No, but we'd like to have a few words with both you and the chemist.'

'Mr Brown is in the dispensary.' She points at the prescriptions counter.

'Wow, what do you make of that?' Sarah whispers as they walk to the dispensary.

'Make of what, Constable?'

'The hair, she's got a Marilyn Monroe hairdo.'

The door behind the prescriptions counter is partly open. Ellington knocks.

'What is it, Catherine?' The voice could be male or female.

'Police Mr Brown. We're here to ask a few questions about Elise Seymour.'

Nathan Brown is a man who matches his name. His hair is brown and bushy, his eyes are brown, he has a lot of brown spots on his face and the collar of a brown shirt peeks out from under his coat. The pungent smell of chemicals tickles Sarah's nose. She hates that smell. It reminds her of that ghastly day when she visited Aaron in hospital, the day he died.

The dispensary is small and pokey, cupboards line two walls and a refrigerator stands near a sink. A table and two chairs are pushed up against the far wall. A small partly opened window provides air, and overhead fluorescent tubes provide light.

'Is she still missing?'

'I'm afraid so. When was the last time you saw her?'

'Wednesday evening. It would have been around six.'

'How had she been that day?'

'What do you mean?'

'Was she her usual self? Did anything out of the ordinary happen?'

'She was very quiet that day, but then, she was always fairly quiet.'

'Did she talk to you about anything that might have been worrying her?'

'No.'

'When she failed to turn up for work yesterday morning, what did you do?'

'Well, I myself was late. I didn't get to the shop until after nine. Catherine had opened up and was in a bit of a state, having to look after everything alone. I was most surprised that Elise hadn't arrived, she was always here before eight-thirty and she often opened up.'

'Everyone had keys to the shop?'

'Yes, I gave keys to both Elise and Catherine.'

'And they are your only employees?'

'That's right.'

'What did you do when Elise didn't arrive?'

'Around ten, I phoned her mobile. When I couldn't get through, I tried phoning her house. I got the engaged signal.'

'What time was that?'

'Just after ten, I tried again around two. I got the engaged signal again.'

'You didn't think to call around to her house. After all, it isn't far away.'

'No, I didn't get a chance during the day, we were rather busy, but I understand Catherine called around there in her lunch break. Then this morning I got the phone call from Mrs Seymour just before nine. That's the first I knew of Elise's disappearance.'

'What sort of an employee was Elise?'

'Very capable, she was intelligent, industrious and very good with the customers. I'm quite upset over her disappearance.'

'Have you ever had contact with Elise away from the shop?'

Brown juts his chin and frowns. 'No. Why do you ask that?'

'We're just trying to build a profile of Elise, find out places she might have visited.'

'Apart from her being an employee in this shop, I know

very little about Elise. She never confided in me over anything.'

'If you think of anything that might assist us, please call,' Ellington hands Brown his card. 'We will need to talk with Catherine.'

'Of course, I'll get her.'

Catherine hovers in the doorway.

'Come in Catherine. We won't take too much of your time.'

'How long have you known Elise?'

'From when she first started here.'

'And when was that?'

'Nearly a year ago, about nine months I think.'

'How did you get on with each other?'

'Good, we were best friends.'

'Oh? So, you met outside of work?'

'Not really. Elise was tied up on weekends with her church, but we did talk a lot when the shop was quiet. We sometimes had a coffee after work.'

'Have you ever met any of Elise's other friends?'

'No, I don't think she had any other friends.'

'When was the last time you saw Elise?'

'Wednesday at six, that's when we locked up and she left. She usually stayed back to help with the tidying up, but Wednesday was different.'

'How was it different?'

'Elise was very sad all day. I think she just wanted to get home.'

'Do you know what caused her sadness?'

'Although she wouldn't talk to me about why she was upset, I know it was that boy that caused it.'

'What boy?'

'The boy she used to be engaged to...Rick.'

'Tell us what happened on Wednesday, Catherine.'

'Well, I got here at about eight twenty. I was pulling the sheets off the tables when I saw Elise and Rick outside the shop, talking. Elise was waving her arms around and then Rick walked off. She was crying when she came in. I asked her what was wrong, but she didn't answer. She just went to the cupboard, put on her coat and changed her shoes. I asked her again. She looked at me real funny and didn't answer. She kept her distance all day and at her lunch break, she didn't go out as she usually did. Instead, she just sat in the dispensary. I came in and made her a cup of coffee. It was still there an hour later, stone cold.'

'Did you usually lunch together?'

'No. We had to have separate lunches. I had my forty minutes break between twelve and twelve forty, then Elise started hers.'

'What was her relationship with Mr Brown?'

Catherine frowns. 'What do you mean?'

'Were they friendly with each other?'

'As far as I know, he was just the boss and she was just the employee. I don't know what you're getting at.' Catherine's small eyes narrow.

'So apart from being quiet and upset, there's nothing else you can tell us about Elise's behaviour on Wednesday?'

'That's right.'

'Then on Thursday morning what time did you arrive here?'

'Same time, about eight twenty. The shop was still closed, I had to open up.'

'Was this unusual?'

'I suppose so, usually Elise or Mr Brown opened up.'

'Then what happened after you opened up?'

'I had to deal with a few customers alone. By nine, I

was really feeling panicked. Elise hadn't arrived and neither had Mr Brown.'

'When did Brown arrive?'

'It was around nine thirty.'

'Was this unusual?'

'Yes, it was. He said he'd had car trouble. When Elise hadn't arrived at ten, I suggested we phone her. Mr Brown tried her mobile and then her home phone. He couldn't raise her. When my lunch break came, I tried to phone Elise myself. No luck. I decided to walk around to her house. I knocked on the front door. When there wasn't an answer, I walked around the side, but the gate to the back garden was locked. I thought I heard something so I called out: *anyone home*? There was no answer so I came back here.'

'I understand Elise gave you her iPad.'

'That's right. She gave it to me soon after she started working here.'

'May I see it?'

Catherine goes to a small cupboard and removes a handbag. She takes out a small iPad and hands it to Ellington.

'Elise deleted everything on it before she gave it to me.'

Ellington flips it open and silently examines the contents.

'Elise is a beautiful person, she's made a big difference to my life,' Catherine whispers.

'In what way?'

'I felt ugly and unwanted. Elise made me feel different. She showed me that even an ugly duckling can have a life. She used to say: *There is beauty in everyone Catherine. Just seek your own beauty and concentrate on that.* She told me where to buy nice clothes, and I loved her hair so much I asked the hairdresser across the road to give me the same style.'

Ellington catches Sarah's smirk. 'You said you and Elise sometimes had coffee after work. Where did you go?'

'The little coffee shop near the car park, there's only one in Summer Hill.'

'Did you meet up with anyone or talk with anyone on these occasions?'

'Only Jeff the waiter.'

'And what sort of conversations did you have with Jeff the waiter?

'We just ordered our coffees.'

'If you think of anything at all that might help us, contact me.' Ellington flips open his wallet and hands the girl his card along with the iPad.

Outside, Ellington surveys the busy street. The smell of freshly brewed coffee attracts Sarah's attention. 'Do you think we ought to talk to Jeff the waiter?' she asks.

'Probably a waste of time.'

'I don't think so.' Sarah leaves Ellington on the footpath and marches towards the coffee shop.   He reluctantly follows her in.

The café is small and dim. The only other customer is a man wearing stubby shorts, a black singlet and heavy work boots. He conscientiously bites into a huge muffin as he reads his paper. Ellington and Sarah sit at a table next to the window. Ellington stares out at the passing parade of pedestrians. 'This is quite a busy centre,' he observes.

'Thought we might as well have a coffee and a snack while we're here, after all, it is nearly midday and I'm starving. I'm having coffee and a muffin. What do you want Sarge?'

'Oh, so Jeff the waiter wasn't the main reason for coming in here eh, Constable?' Ellington consults his watch and acknowledges silently to himself that he could do with a coffee hit.

Missing In Red

A thin blonde girl with colourful tattooed arms takes their orders. 'Won't be long.' she mutters.

The coffees and muffins come together. Ellington looks up at the waitress. 'I'd like to talk with Jeff.'

'He starts at five.'

Ellington opens the album. 'Do you know this girl?'

The waitress peers closely at the photo, her eyes open widely. 'Blimey, who is *that*?'

'A local girl who's gone missing.' Ellington doesn't bother with his ID or a formal introduction. Sarah's in uniform, that'll do.

'Never seen her before, if I had, I sure wouldn't forget. Looks like a movie star.' The girl takes one last lingering look at the photo shaking her head. 'Sorry'.

'Are you sure? Her name's Elise Seymour, she works at the chemist's.'

'I'm only a casual, I'm not here often. They call me in when they're short of staff. Today it's only me, and the barista. Come at five if you want to catch Jeff.'

Sarah takes a sip of her coffee and says: 'Tell me what you found in Elise's phone.'

Ellington takes out the mobile and flicks it open. 'Here's a text message.' He reads it aloud. *You know where Rick is. Tell me bitch or you'll be sorry. Tara.'*

'Charming.'

'The call came in on Tuesday night and Elise disappears on Thursday morning. We'll be having a talk with this Tara.'

'Anything else there?'

Ellington squints into the phone as he searches. 'Nope.'

'A beautiful tall blonde in a bright red dress would surely attract someone's attention.'

Sarah takes another sip of her coffee. 'People can be unbelievably unaware, and all the people I spoke to out there were not exactly in the spring of their lives.'

'Agreed, the lot I talked to were all very senior. Maybe we should chat with some of the other shopkeepers.'

'That we will, constable.' Ellington looks at his muffin. 'Why are they so big?'

'I'm sure you can manage it.'

Ellington takes a bite and chews slowly. 'It's pretty obvious why we were marched into action so early.'

'Why?'

'David Seymour holds the balance of power in a Bill being debated in Parliament. If it goes through, a lot of State Police power will be compromised. The big brass doesn't want that, and they're keeping sweet with Seymour, doing everything they can to find his daughter, making sure his vote goes the right way.'

'I thought it was over the top sending a senior detective to find a person who'd been missing less than a day,' Sarah murmurs.

He nods at Sarah's empty cup, 'ready to go?'

They tackle the shopkeepers together. The fruit shop is first on the list. A short squat man with tanned skin and unruly black hair hums as he arranges a stack of apples.

'You here about the rascal who's been stealing stuff off the dry cleaner?' He glances at Ellington and continues his stacking.

'No. We're looking for this girl.' Ellington shows the man Elise's picture. A smile spreads widely across his face as he stares at the photo. 'She's lovely, so pretty.' He kisses the tips of his fingers. 'Every time I see her, I wish I was thirty again!' he laughs. 'So, where she go?'

'That's what we're trying to find out. When did you last

see Elise Seymour, sir?'

'Wednesday morning. She talked to a fella outside the chemist.'

'Anything at all you can tell us that might help us find Elise?'

'Sorry'. He sadly shakes his head.

The newsagent and dry cleaner remember Elise only as a quiet, irregular customer.

The hairdresser's salon is long and narrow. The sweet smell of hairspray mingles with the sharp acrid smell of nail acrylic. A middle-aged woman is daintily clipping scissors over a client's grey head, and a younger one is at a table working on a pair of hands. Both stop their tasks when Ellington and Sarah walk in. Ellington approaches the nail therapist and shows his ID. 'Detective Sergeant Ellington.'

The girl stares at Ellington with fearful eyes. 'What's happened?'

'We're investigating the disappearance of a young woman.' He opens the album and places it on the one free spot he can find on the messy table. 'Do you recognise her?'

The girl's face relaxes. 'For a minute I thought you had some bad news about my brother, he's gone missing too.'

'Have you reported this?'

'Oh yeah, he's been missing two years.' She studies the photo. 'She's a client...Elise.'

'When did you last see her?'

'Four, maybe five weeks ago, I can look up my appointments book. She came in for her nails and hair.'

'You haven't seen her in the last few days?'

'Can't say I have.'

The woman with the scissors listens intently. Sarah approaches her. 'When did *you* last see Elise Seymour?'

'The same day Jackie saw her. I cut her hair.'

'How often did she come here?'

'Like Jackie said, about once a month. Not as often as before though.'

'Before?'

'Before, when she was having her hair dyed.'

'I don't understand. Her hair was quite fair in recent pictures.'

'That was her natural colour. She used to come in here to have her hair dyed black.'

'Did she confide in you about why she changed her hair back to blonde?'

'It had something to do with her becoming a Christian. Well, that's what she told me.'

The real estate agent, dentist, cake shop, hotel and supermarket have nothing to offer.

The butcher's shop had been crowded every time they passed, but at last, they find him with only one customer. The man whistles happily as he wraps some meat. He winks and grins as he hands his elderly female customer a parcel. 'Now you have a good day, my lovely.'

Sarah nudges Ellington and whispers in his ear: 'He's obviously been to butchers' charm school.'

Ellington frowns, he has no idea what Sarah's talking about. The butcher has no difficulty placing Elise Seymour. 'Sure, I know her. Best looking gal in town.' He winks at Sarah, she winks back. His eyes widen, he wasn't expecting *that* from the little police girl.

'When did you last see her?' Ellington asks tersely.

'Would have been Wednesday, yes Wednesday, I saw her walking by around six.'

'Anything at all you can tell me that might help us find her?'

'Not really, we never actually got talking. She'd come

in once or twice a week. This is a busy shop, not much time for chatting.'

On the drive back to the station, Sarah picks up one of Ellington's cards from the consul. She cocks her head to one side as she reads. 'Your name is Luke, why does everyone call you Duke?'

'I've always been called Duke.'

'Why? Luke is such a nice name.'

'Long story.'

'I like long stories, tell me.'

Ellington shrugs and narrows his eyes as the memories crowd in. 'It started at school. There was a famous musician, decades ago, called Duke Ellington. Luke rhymes with Duke, so that's what I got called.'

'You're not at school anymore.'

'The same happened when I joined the Force. I guess people still remember Duke Ellington.'

'I've never heard of him, and I prefer Luke.'

'Well, you can call me Sarge.'

CHAPTER 5

Ellington stands waiting at Bellamy's open door. His chief is barking into the phone. 'For Christ's sake, can't you follow orders?' Looking up, Bellamy motions with a hand for Ellington to enter. 'I expect some sort of a report by four this afternoon.' He slams the phone down and glares at Ellington with wide eyes and raised eyebrows.

'I've interviewed the Seymours. Their daughter's disappearance is out of character and a massive shock to them. There's nothing to suggest she ran off somewhere without telling them. I spoke to her employer, the local chemist Nathan Brown and the other employee, Catherine Brennan. Nothing there apart from Catherine mentioning that Elise was upset the day before she disappeared. Apparently, she met up with her ex-fiancé that morning, and there was an altercation. We interviewed shopkeepers and residents in the area, again nothing.' Ellington moves towards Bellamy's desk. 'But one resident found Elise Seymour's mobile phone in the gutter outside his house.' Ellington takes the phone from his pocket and plonks it on the desk. 'All call and message history has been deleted except for one message which came in two nights before she went missing.'

'Tell me.'

'From Tara Gresham.'

Missing In Red

'Who is Tara Gresham, and what's the message?'

'Tara Gresham is an ex-friend of Elise Seymour's, she's also the ex-girlfriend of Elise Seymour's ex-fiancé.'

'I'm sorry I asked. What's the message?'

Ellington recalls the message without referring back to the phone: *You know where Rick is. Tell me bitch, or you'll be sorry.* She was referring to Richard Ballantyne, Elise Seymour's ex-fiancé.'

'Could the phone have been dropped deliberately?'

'Possibly, or she could have accidentally dropped it. On the other hand, she might have been trying to send a message and was interrupted.'

'What's your next step?'

'I'll be talking with Tara Gresham.'

'Good. Keep me informed.'

Ellington wrestles with the idea of interviewing Tara Gresham that day, but decides it's too late. He'll do it next week.

*

A rainy Saturday is sufficient enticement for Ellington to stay indoors and read Elise Seymour's diary. The first month is in code, and the first legible entry is:

February 1: *I seem to be constantly living in the past. Today I went back nearly three years thinking about my darling grandmother and the sadness I felt when she died. Mother had just found out about my shoulder tattoo and was in a rotten mood. She told me Nana had had a stroke and was not expected to live. She carried on about how upset she was. How hypocritical! She hadn't spoken with Nana in nine years. I really loved my grandmother. She told me stories and played scrabble with me. She had the sweetest smile and her hair was white and wavy. She must have loved me too. She left me thirty thousand dollars. They wanted me to put the money into an annuity or shares. I defied them and bought my Toyota ....my purple people eater.*

More coding follows interspersed with occasional written entries.

March 4: *To please mother I wore my watermelon pink to church today. She spent such time making it I felt I should show my appreciation. It's three months now since my heart broke, but I know I have to get on with my life. I have applied for a job with the local chemist. What a come down! There's been more upheaval in my life, but I have to watch what I tell you dear diary, and maybe I shouldn't record those events here. There could be spies around.*

March 8: *My application was successful and I have met my new employer, Nathan Brown. A girl, Catherine Brennan works there also. I think she's backward, probably developmentally disabled. This is a challenge, maybe I can help her.*

March 31: *Work was tedious as usual, but I do enjoy helping in the dispensary. Catherine raved about my frock and I expect in the near future she'll turn up with something similar after much searching through every vintage shop in the city.*

Ellington takes another sip of his coffee. The coding continues until April 12: *He passed this morning with his nose in the air. Why can't I stop loving him? In my lunch break, I took a walk to their house. The garden was a mess. I could have made it so lovely. I looked through the side window and saw their bed. I vomited in their garden.*

May 3: *Gregory Allenby phoned me at the shop. He's becoming a problem. I'm running out of excuses. Mother keeps pushing me in his direction. Nathan Brown is another one, he can't keep his hands to himself. If only these people knew how repulsive they are.*

Ellington takes a bite of his biscuit and strokes his temple. His thoughts are flying, so Pastor Allenby and the chemist were both making lines for Elise. The next fifty-two pages are covered in numbers and symbols until June.

June 14:   *Catherine is driving me ballistic. I try my hardest to be kind to her, but she's becoming so possessive I'll have to start distancing myself.*

August 16: *Things are getting sticky. Gregory just can't write sermons, he's hopeless. He will lose the whole congregation if it continues like this.   I don't know what happened in Dunkley. He won't talk about it. Maybe he was thrown out because of his dreadful sermons. I have offered to help. I know what the people want.*

September 17: *I have agreed to help Gregory with his sermons starting from today. He wants me to come to the parsonage. I suggested I email them to him. He insists on my coming over, said it's important to discuss them personally. He's asked me not to tell anyone, said people might talk. He wants me to go over Tuesdays and Fridays, leave Mrs Tingwell early. He begged me, said it was my duty. I don't know what to do.*

September 22: *I try not to feel bad leaving Mrs Tingwell early. I make sure she has her dinner and is settled. She usually falls asleep in front of the TV anyway. Gregory cooked me a nice dinner and then we discussed the sermon. I've promised not to mention any of this to anyone. He said it would demean him. I can see his point.*

October 4:   *the church people are treating me like a saint. Sometimes I feel as if I have been sent by God to help them. In fact, I know I've been on earth many times before. I feel strongly that in one of my past lives, I was an Egyptian Princess. Another life I remember was when I was Mary, the mother of Jesus. I clearly remember when the Angel came and asked me if I would agree to be the mother of the Son of God. I agreed with great joy.*

Ellington shakes his head. The girl had been diagnosed with bipolar. It's clear from this last entry, her mental state was declining and she was having delusions. He reads on.

October 15: *I am being inspired by God to write perfect sermons. They are uplifting and beautiful. I can't take the credit. It's God's spirit within me that's creating these wonderful homilies. I have been given a great gift and I must use it to help others. I pray every day that Rick and I will be reunited. I know it will happen soon.*

The rest of the diary is coded. It's clear to Ellington the girl was in some sort of trouble. The Department's coding expert Doug Barnes will be needed on this one.

*

Sunday dawns bright and very warm. Ellington pulls out his *funerals and weddings* suit and chooses a tie. When he can't find a laundered dress shirt, he bundles the suit back into the wardrobe and selects light casual slacks and a checked sports shirt.

The Church of Jesus and his Saints is a modest weatherboard cottage standing on a corner lot only a block away from the impressive brick and tile Anglican Church. Twenty or so cars line the street and three are parked on the front lawn. Ellington leaves his car in a back street and walks slowly to his destination. He is irritated to hear singing as he approaches the front doorway. His watch tells him it's ten after eleven. He had hoped the service would be well and truly finished by now.

The room is packed with close to fifty people. Ellington stands at the back trying to block out the raucous, discordant singing. A thin man in a grey cassock stands at the front,

74

raising limp hands in an effort to conduct, and a silver-haired woman thumps at the piano struggling to keep in time with the roaming voices. Sunlight streams through the louvred shutters casting yellow stripes across the unadorned altar table. It's oppressively hot, and the current created by the lone ceiling fan is totally inadequate. Ellington cynically considers the congregation. The numbers severely ignore the Covid-19 laws on social distancing. No wonder Seymour tried to dissuade him from coming here.

When the hymn finishes, Pastor Allenby speaks, his voice deep and booming. 'We must continue to pray for our dear daughter Elise, and beg the Lord to deliver her back to us unharmed and in good health.' He spreads his arms outwards. 'Now let us join together in friendship and fellowship.'

As people begin to mingle, David Seymour makes his way to Ellington. 'Welcome to our little church, detective. They'll be bringing tea out shortly.'

'I take it you've heard nothing from your daughter?'

Seymour shakes his head mournfully. 'Nothing. What about you? What are you doing to find her?'

'I've interviewed the pharmacist, the other employee Catherine Brennan, shopkeepers and nearby residents.'

'And?'

'Nothing from them so far, but we did find her mobile.'

Seymour's eyes widen. 'You have, where?'

'Hamilton Street. It was in the gutter in front of fifty-six.'

'Oh God, that doesn't sound good.'

'Did you know that most of Elise's diary entries were in code?'

'How could I? I don't read her diary.'

'Elise felt someone was reading it.'

'No one but Janet and I have access to her room.'

Seymour takes a handkerchief from his pocket and wipes it across his forehead. 'Come out to the garden, it's cooler.'

Apart from a few scraggly azaleas growing on the back perimeter, there is no garden to speak of. A few chairs and a garden seat, all occupied by elderly women, sink into the damp overgrown grass.

Ellington and Seymour find a spot of shade beneath an ancient gum. They watch Pastor Allenby as he makes his way across the yard toward them. His thinning grey hair and gaunt features make it hard to assess his age. Ellington makes a guess at mid-fifties.

'Welcome David, any news of Elise?' Allenby offers his hand to David Seymour.

'Gregory, meet Detective Sergeant Ellington. He's in charge of the investigation.'

'What have you found so far detective?'

'Not a great deal. It's quite a mystery at this point. It seems no one saw Elise after she left her home Thursday morning. She seems to have vanished into thin air. When was the last time you saw her sir?'

'Last Sunday, right here.'

'No contact at all since then?'

'None whatsoever.'

'I understand Elise helped you with your sermons.'

Allenby's eyebrows shoot up and his jaw clenches. 'Who told you that?'

'Elise wrote it in her diary. Did she ever confide in you about her personal problems?'

'Never. In fact, apart from the two or three times she helped me with my sermons we had no contact.' The man's eyes dart around the yard. 'I must move on. Do everything in your power to bring our little saint back home. She is desperately missed.'

As Allenby turns to go, Ellington holds up his hand, 'just a moment sir. I must advise you that you and your congregation are breaking the Covid 19 social distancing law currently existing in this State. I won't make any charges today but you must take this as a warning. For that room to comply with the law, numbers should not exceed twenty people.' Ellington nods his head towards the house.

Allenby's eyes widen. 'Detective, these people rely on our Sunday services. For some of them, it's the only thing that keeps them going, and of course, they are all vaccinated.'

'You can have two services.'

'These people come together as a family. I wouldn't know how to separate them.'

'The only way you can have this number at the same time is to have some inside the house and some out here in the yard.' Ellington sighs loudly. 'Look, it's not for me to tell you how to do it. But if you don't comply with this order, charges will be laid against you and the people in attendance.'

'We'll work something out, Gregory,' Seymour says gently. Allenby nods and moves away. The grey cassock melts into the crowded yard as an elderly woman juggling a full tray approaches them. Her legs are bowed, and she walks with a pronounced limp. Her silvery hair frames a face bearing nearly a hundred years of wrinkles. She speaks in a wavering croak. 'Poor Mr Seymour, you must be out of your mind. Take a cuppa.' The woman pushes the tray towards Seymour.

'Thank you. Mrs Wright, this is Detective Ellington. He's helping us find Elise.'

'Oh Detective, you must find our angel. She is everything to us. Please have some tea, scones are on their way.' Ellington takes a cup.

'When did you last see Elise, Mrs Wright?'

'Last Sunday in this very church, she looked so

beautiful in her lovely red dress.'

'Did she seem her normal self?'

'Oh yes, the same as always, calm, peaceful, holy. She was very holy.'

'In what way?'

'Like a saint. Like the saints you read about in the Bible. I must move on or the tea will get cold. Please find our little angel, detective.'

As Mrs Wright moves off, another elderly woman joins them.

'Mr Seymour, I've just been talking to your wife. I told her and I'm telling you, if there's anything at all we can do for you in this worrying time, please let me know.'

'That's very kind of you. Esther, meet Detective Ellington. He's helping us find Elise. Detective this is Esther Raymond.'

Esther seems even older than Mrs Wright. A floral pink dress hangs loosely on her thin, bony frame. Her tiny face is almost lost behind clouds of white hair puffing out in wild disarray. 'You must find her. We will all be lost without her. She does so much for us older people. Did you know she goes every Tuesday and Friday night to help Maude Tingwell? And on Saturdays, she takes two of us shopping. That's true charity. You don't see it too often Mr Ellington, and when it comes on your doorstep, it's a great blessing.'

'Quite right Mrs Raymond. Were you here last Sunday?' The woman draws in her breath as if outraged by the question.

'Of course, one doesn't miss church.'

'Of course not, did you speak with Elise?'

'Naturally, we all make a point of speaking with Elise. She's so wise for her years it's as if she's been here before.'

'How do you mean?'

'Like God has sent her specially.'

Ellington scratches his chin. The conversations are starting to frazzle him.

'Did she take you shopping last Saturday?'

'She definitely did.'

'Did anything at all happen out of the ordinary?'

'Whatever do you mean?' The woman's mouth forms a cross little beak and she reminds Ellington of a small ruffled parrot. A short, smiling, red-cheeked woman appears with a plate of buttered scones. 'I believe you're looking for our Elise,' the newcomer wheezes.

'Marion, this is Detective Ellington.'

'Elise is okay. I'm sure. God is with her.'

'When did you last see Elise, Marion?' Ellington asks.

'Sunday, Elise was in her element. She explained to us the true meaning of the parable of the loaves and fishes.'

'That isn't a parable Marion,' Esther interrupts indignantly. 'That really happened.'

'Well anyway, Elise is an expert on the bible. She knows it from front to back. And as for the Ten Commandments, I know she has never broken any of them.'

'How do you know that?' Ellington tries to hide his cynicism.

'She told me. She also told me that she had been sent to us by God to guide us to perfection so that we will inherit the kingdom.'

Ellington stuffs a small scone into his mouth and chews it quickly. 'Did she take you shopping on Saturdays?'

'Oh no, I can do my own shopping. It was mainly Esther here...' she glances towards Esther, 'and Joan Haywood, Elise takes shopping. Have another scone Detective. David?'

'If you stay any longer Marion, I'll eat them all,' David smiles.

Missing In Red

'Well, I'd better move on. God will deliver her, mark my words.' The two women move off in different directions.

'I'll need to talk to the other lady Elise takes shopping. I'll also need to talk to the one Elise visits on Tuesdays and Fridays.'

'Maude Tingwell doesn't come to church anymore, she's too debilitated. Her address will be in that book you found in Elise's room.' David takes a sip of tea. 'I didn't know Elise was helping Pastor Allenby with his sermons. I thought it was just his accounts.'

In the next hour, Ellington talks with several people including Joan Haywood. All have Elise on a saintly pedestal but none have anything to say that helps his investigation.

He approaches Janet Seymour. 'I'd like to take another look in Elise's room. Would it be okay if I call in after this?'

'I suppose so.' The reply is brusque.

'No need to rush away, just leave when you're ready. I'll sit in my car. I can read the Sunday papers while I'm waiting.' He forces a slight smile.

Ellington parks outside the Seymour house. He is only on page two of the newspaper when the Seymour's car pulls into the garage. He waits a few minutes before approaching the front door. Seymour opens it before Ellington has a chance to knock. 'Come in.' He leads Ellington to the lounge room. Janet Seymour is sitting in almost the same position as she was on Friday. She speaks in a low mournful voice. 'You saw detective, how she is loved. The devotion those people show Elise is just incredible. She's a saint to them, a holy person who does no wrong.'

'The girl who works at the pharmacy said Elise seemed quite upset last Wednesday. How was she that night, here?' Ellington asks.

Janet draws in her breath before speaking. 'She got

80

home a little earlier than usual, so we had dinner around seven. She picked at her food, hardly spoke. She went off to her room soon after, said she was tired and needed an early night.'

'May I see her room again?'

Janet shrugs unhappily. David Seymour moves towards the hallway. Ellington puts up a restraining hand. 'I can find my way there, thanks.'

As Ellington enters the room, he is immediately engulfed in its intoxicating atmosphere. The overpowering fragrance, the orderliness and the ambience engulf him. He can almost feel her presence. He opens the wardrobe and brushes his hand along the line of dresses. He's not quite sure what he's looking for but feels strongly that the answer lies here in this room. He pulls open the drawers one by one. Nothing has changed, everything is still in perfect order. Everything from the stack of silky underwear to the neatly folded nightgowns. At that moment a strange sensation takes hold of him. It's as if he knows Elise Seymour intimately, that he has a real connection with her. He flinches as the gruesome sight of Melanie Churchill's mutilated body flashes into his brain. Nothing like that can happen to Elise Seymour. A determination settles in his mind. He *will* find her.

Back home, Ellington continues reading the two major Sunday papers. They have both run a story on Elise Seymour's disappearance along with her photograph.

*

Ellington is in his office before nine, unusual for a Monday, but he has lots to do. He left a message for Doug Barnes the coding expert and is now looking up estate agents in Croydon. There is only one.

'Globe 50, Katie speaking. How can I help you?' A high-pitched, nasally voice chirps.

'I'm looking for Richard Ballantyne. I believe he might be employed there?'

'That's right. He works here, but I'm afraid he's not in the office right now. He should be back around ten.'

'Thanks. I'll call then.'

'How was church?' The voice is soft.

Ellington swivels his chair around and faces Sarah's mocking grin.

'It helped me remember why I don't go anymore.'

'That bad?'

'I met a lot of old dears who think Elise Seymour should be canonised.'

'What about the pastor?'

'Not much from him, except he's lying.'

'What about?'

'In her diary, Elise wrote things about Allenby, stuff he lied about.'

'What things?'

'Elise had been going to his house for months writing his sermons. Allenby lied about that and said she'd only been there a couple of times.'

'Why was she writing his sermons?'

'Because he couldn't.'

'Couldn't?'

'According to the diary, Allenby's sermons were rubbish.'

'What else was in the diary?'

'There's a lot in code. I'm getting Doug Barnes on the job.'

'If Doug can't decode it, no one can.'

'Right, stick around, I'll be talking with Richard Ballantyne today and I'll need you.'

'Great to be needed.'

'Something else you can do.' He hands Sarah the slip of paper David Seymour had given him. 'Check Elise's bank account. Get me a run down.'

Bellamy shouts across the office. 'Channel Seven is sending a crew out this morning. They want to interview you. They're going to the Seymour house first to interview Mr and Mrs.'

*

The Chanel Seven crew sets up in Bellamy's office. Brett Hudson, a well-known journalist briefs Ellington on the questions he'll be asking. 'I'll ask you how you're proceeding with the investigation and if you believe there's been foul play.'

'That all?'

'I'll touch on Elise's background, although the interview with the parents pretty well covered that.'

'How *did* it go with the Seymours?' Ellington asks.

'Those sorts of interviews are always hard. The mother's a mess and the father like a piece of stone, but I got what I wanted for the viewers.' He glances across to the cameraman, 'Looks like we're ready to shoot.'

The interview is over in a few minutes. Only one take was needed.

CHAPTER 6

Globe 50 Real Estate is directly opposite Croydon railway station. Its glass facade is crowded with numerous photographs of properties for sale. Richard Ballantyne's office is small and cramped. It's one of three small offices running off the reception area. Sarah can immediately see why Ballantyne is such a ladies' man. He is tall and well built, his sharply chiselled jaw sprouts fashionable stubble and his welcoming smile displays two rows of perfect white teeth.

'No, I had no idea Elise had gone missing.' He runs his hand through thick dark hair.

'Didn't read yesterday's papers?' Ellington quizzes.

'As a matter of fact, I didn't get around to it. I was busy settling into my new digs.'

'Have you any idea where Elise might be?'

'None at all.'

'When was the last time you spoke with her?'

'Wednesday morning.'

Ellington's eyes narrow. 'Tell me what was said.'

Ballantyne closes his eyes for a few seconds. When he opens them, he looks past Ellington and fixes them on Sarah. 'I was surprised to see Elise standing outside the chemist shop. Apparently, she'd been waiting for me.'

'And?'

He looks from Sarah to Ellington. 'She asked me to come back to her.'

'We've been told you'd been separated for twelve months. Was this the first time she'd contacted you in that time?'

'Quite often in the early days after the separation, she would call, but in the past nine or so months we hadn't spoken at all.' Ballantyne looks at his hands and takes a deep breath.

'Why did she make this particular contact?' Ellington asks.

'My ex-girlfriend Tara, had apparently told her we'd broken up. That's why Elise wanted to talk.'

'Elise thought that because you were through with Tara, you might come back to her?' Sarah asks.

'Yes exactly. I made it clear that I didn't want to start again, that I was taking an overseas trip and would probably be away a few years.'

'What was her reaction?'

'I didn't hang around to find out. I had to go. I had my train to catch.'

'You haven't spoken to her since?' Ellington asks.

'No.'

'We're trying to build a profile of Elise. I need to know as much about her as I can.' Ellington stares into the blue-green eyes. 'I need to know her personality, her likes, dislikes, moods, friends, everything.'

'She's a very insecure girl. She desperately wants to please, and she does whatever she can to please.'

'Can you give me an example?'

'When I said I'd love a motorcycle, she bought me one.'

'There's a photo of Elise sitting on a motorbike. Is that the bike?'

85

'Yes. I took that photo.'

'Quite a big bike looks like a Harley.'

'It *is* a Harley.'

'How could a young girl afford a bike like that?'

'A few months earlier, she'd come into an inheritance from her grandmother and bought herself a car. When I said I'd like a bike, she sold the car to Tara and bought me the bike.'

'Where's the bike now?'

'Where I'm staying.'

'You've still got it?'

'She said she didn't want it back.'

Ellington and Sarah exchange glances. Ellington clears his throat and stares steadily at Ballantyne. 'You travel to work by train, any reason you don't ride your bike?'

'No need. I live five minutes from the train, and this end...' He waves his arm towards the window. 'Well, you saw the station, just across the road. If I have to visit a client, I take one of the company cars.'

'You don't own a car?'

'I do actually. I've had a car for years, an old Ford.'

'Mrs Seymour thinks that the Elise you were engaged to, wasn't the real Elise. She thinks Elise only put on the tough act to fit in with you and your friends.'

'As I said before, Elise always wanted to please, but I knew her too well. That blonde bimbo look is not Elise. I think she adopted that just to please her mother.'

'Did you know Elise was bipolar?'

'Yes, but so are lots of people.'

'When were you first aware?'

'A couple of years ago, we'd only been engaged a few weeks. Then out of the blue, she started saying weird things.'

'What sort of weird things?'

'Like, aliens were controlling her brain.' Ballantyne shakes his head slowly. 'Then she would start talking to someone, but no one was there. It was scary. I asked her who she was talking to. She said there was someone in her head telling her to do bad things. She said she was telling him to get lost.'

'Was she on drugs?'

'Not really, we had the odd hit, nothing much at all.' Ballantyne squeezes his eyes shut. 'One night she started crying, over nothing. She cried for hours. I couldn't pacify her. I felt helpless. I told her father and said I think he should take her to a doctor.' Ballantyne widens his eyes and stares towards the window. 'At first, the doctor said she had schizophrenia, but eventually, she was diagnosed with bipolar. She started on Prozac. That seemed to help, but although she didn't hear voices or any of that shit, she still wasn't right.'

'In what way?'

'In her head, she had severe moods...She swung from being outgoing and happy to miserable and depressed in the space of a few minutes. I put up with that for another year.'

'The parents say Elise was only diagnosed with bipolar when you left her.'

'They would say that, wouldn't they? Elise went to Doc Horton. He'll tell you when she was diagnosed. Those parents are a pair of controllers.' Ballantyne takes a deep breath before speaking again. 'I loved Elise for three years then I stopped loving her. She started irritating me. Her highs and lows were too hard to handle.'

'Was that when you turned to Tara, your best mate's girlfriend?'

'Tara didn't love Travis. She used him, just like she tried to use me.'

'What happened when you told Elise you wanted to break off with her?'

Ballantyne looks into his hands and sighs heavily. 'It was awful. She cried and begged and pleaded. I had to be strong.'

Sarah rolls her eyes to Ellington.

'When did you and Tara break up?' she asks.

'Just last week, I packed up and left.'

'Where are you living now? Sarah asks.

'I'm staying with a mate. Someone Tara doesn't know.'

'She knows where you work, I presume.'

'Yes, but I've left instructions with Katie not to put her through if she phones.'

'Elise knew where you and Tara lived. Did she ever contact you there?' Sarah prods.

'She called in one Sunday afternoon, soon after the breakup. She came with gifts. Can you believe, gifts? Naturally it made us both feel like shit, but I think she was having one of her episodes. She was weird. We poured her a drink then she asked for another. After three drinks, I offered to drive her home. She said she was okay, got up and left.'

'Did she and Tara have any contact after that?'

'None that I know of, but of course, Tara doesn't tell me everything, as I recently found out.'

'Like what?'

'Nothing to do with Elise, personal.'

Ellington takes out his notebook. What's the address you're at now?'

'16 Hayes Street Summer Hill.'

'And the one with Tara?'

'29 Stewart Street.'

'Mobile?'

Ballantyne pulls out his wallet and flips out a business

card. Ellington finishes scribbling and takes the card. He then takes a card from his wallet and hands it to Ballantyne. At the door, he turns. 'If you think of anything at all Mr Ballantyne, please call me.'

As Sarah slides into the car, she murmurs. 'Well, I agree with the Seymours, Rick Ballantyne is definitely conceited.'

Ellington nods in agreement and puts the car into motion. 'How did you get on with Elise's account?'

'Last used tenth November, five days before she disappeared, she withdrew one hundred dollars, nothing since then. Her salary from Brown went in the previous Friday.'

CHAPTER 7

Rick Ballantyne stands at the window watching Ellington and Sarah drive off. He'd told them all he wanted to, but not everything. His mind travels back four years, back to the day he met Elise. He thinks about all the things that had happened over those years, including things that Elise and Tara had told him.

2017

He met Elise at an inter-district tennis tournament. She was partnering one of the guys from the local tennis club, and he was playing with his current girlfriend, Sienna.

When Elise walked onto the court in her little white dress, he thought he was having a vision. She was the most beautiful girl he'd ever seen. They introduced themselves at the net and those blue eyes and dimpled cheeks won him totally. He decided there and then, he would add her to his collection. He was very aware of his own good looks. Girls had been queuing for him since he was fifteen. Now at the ripe age of twenty-three, he was highly experienced and knew all there was to know about girls and what they liked.

His attention was hardly on the game, and he double-faulted six times. Elise and her partner won the set easily, six games to two.

'That was a great game you played, Elise. Can I buy

you a coke?'

'The winners buy the drinks, Rick,' she smiled.

'Sorry, but we can't stay. We're off to a party.' Sienna's voice was cold and unfriendly. She was fighting mad. Apart from the fact that Rick had played shit tennis, she was quite aware of the way he was looking at the girl. They'd have drinks with Elise over Sienna's dead body. She gave him a defiant stare and stormed off.

He grinned sheepishly. 'Sorry, I forgot about the party. I'd really like to see you again Elise. Got a phone number?'

'I was about to say it's in the book, but since my dad got into politics, our number's silent.'

'Coming Rick?' Sienna screeched.

'Just tell me, I'll remember it.'

Elise told him the number.

'I'll call you tomorrow.'

Sienna was sitting in the passenger's seat tapping her fingers on the consul. He reached across her, pulled a notebook from the glove box, and wrote.

'Got the chick's number, I see.' Sienna's voice was icy.

*

He made the promised call, and from that moment on, he and Elise were an item. On their first date, he took her to the movies. He made sure he was smartly dressed and called for her on time.

'Mum, this is Richard. Rick.'

'How do you do?' Janet Seymour's voice dripped icy formality.

'Hi Mrs Seymour, pleased to meet you.' He offered his hand. Janet limply returned hers.

'What movie are you seeing?'

'It's a remake of a nineteen-sixties movie, *"Bend of the River"* a sort of cowboy movie, I think. You might have seen

91

the original.'

Janet Seymour stiffened. 'I hardly think so, I wasn't born until nineteen seventy-two.'

'Oops, I meant you might have seen a re-run of the original.'

'I didn't. What time does it finish?'

'I'm not certain, probably around ten thirty.'

'Well make sure you have Elise back here by eleven. And when you drop her home, park your car beneath the street light in front of this house.'

'Mum!' Elise was totally embarrassed.

It was just before eleven when he parked under the street light. The car's interior lit up like a Christmas tree. He could feel Janet Seymour's eyes watching his every move. He satisfied himself with a gentle kiss and a hug which delighted Elise but left a definite longing in his nether regions.

Although he tried drowning Janet Seymour in his charm, the woman remained entirely unimpressed. Elise had told him some of her mother's comments. It was clear Janet Seymour wanted to destroy the relationship.

'He's too old for you, Elise,' Janet had said.

'He's only twenty-three.'

'He doesn't act like it.'

'What do you mean?'

'He's a know-it-all. He's been around, I can tell. Just you be careful. If he gets you pregnant, don't come running to me. You won't be allowed in this house.'

'Mum!' Elise was indignant. How could her mother even think such a thing! Elise had only dated kids from school. He made those boys look just like that...boys. He was a real man.

The second date was different. He drove to an isolated spot overlooking the river. He kissed her gently. 'I'm falling in love with you, Elise.'

'Oh Rick. I already love you,' she whispered.

He had learned long ago, that if you want decent sex in a car, you can't have it sitting up. It took a week's wage organising a fully reclining mechanism fitted to the front seat. Over time, this had been worth every cent. With a pull on the handle, the seat reclined back. Elise laughed, 'That's clever.'

'It's more comfortable,' he grinned. He kissed her again. When his hand touched her breast, Elise didn't resist. She only kissed him harder. He gently pulled off her blouse and buried his head on her chest sucking her nipples. Elise's groan of pleasure encouraged him to send his hand up her skirt and into her underwear. His fingers caressed gently, patiently. Elise's sighing and wetness urged him on. He expertly removed her panties and rolled onto her. Now Elise was feeling more than his fingers.

'Rick, no. I might get pregnant.'

'You're not on the pill?'

'No. I've never done this before.'

It was years since he had been with a girl not on the pill, much less a virgin. He remembered he'd once kept a packet of condoms in the glove box. Would they be still there? It was such a long time since he'd used one. 'Hang on,' he muttered. He searched through the glove box. It was stuffed almost full, with a box of tissues, a notebook, a first aid kit, an Owner's Manual, a packet of mints, sunglasses, a roll of tape, a screwdriver and bingo, a packet of condoms. Elise watched fascinated as he rolled the condom over his engorged organ. She had never seen an erect penis before, and amazed at its size, wondered how it would ever fit in, but her excitement overcame all doubts, and she happily parted her legs to him. He tucked her skirt under her bottom, no point getting bloodstains on the car's good upholstery.

Missing In Red

When he broke her hymen, Elise's cry was short and sharp. Undeterred and driven by single-minded lust he continued thrusting and grunting until he reached a long and satisfying climax. He lay panting, relishing the aftermath, before turning to her. 'I'm sorry if I hurt you, Elise.'

She smiled. 'Let's do it again.'

*

He introduced her to his friends, Travis and Tara, Emmet and Courtney. They were different from the people Elise had mixed with at school. Tara confident and glib had adopted a gothic image. Straight black hair fell to her waist, colourful tattoos covered her body, and a silver ring hung from her nose. Her way-out, slinky clothing contrasted vastly with Elise's plain tops and skirts. Janet had lamented Elise's choice of clothing in recent years and had tried to dress her in the same fancy regalia she'd worn as a kid. Elise rebelled. 'You can't make me wear those things, mum. I'll be a laughing stock. No one dresses like that today.'

Elise couldn't get enough of him and would have preferred to have him all to herself, but when he made it clear he wanted his friends around, she didn't object. She would do anything for him and he knew it. He was also becoming increasingly aware of how Elise was attracting male attention. He didn't like it. It came to a head when the gang went to a local pub one Sunday afternoon. There was a rock group playing, and the place was packed. A guy in a leather jacket was eyeing Elise.

He wandered over. 'Like to dance?' he asked. Elise looked up uncertainly.

With eyes averted Rick said: 'fuck off.'

'I'm talking to the lady. Like to dance beautiful?'

'You heard, fuck off.' Rick growled angrily.

'What do you think, beautiful?' The man asked.

'I'm with my husband,' she lied.

After that, he decided things had to change. Elise was attracting too much attention...attention away from him.

'Looking forward to the rock festival?' he casually asked.

'Absolutely.'

'You'll have to be careful.'

'What do you mean?'

'Well, the way you dress could attract unwanted attention.'

'I don't understand.' Elise blinked.

'Elise, I love you but you're not cool.'

'Cool?'

'Tara's cool. You still look like a school girl with your blonde curls and your plain clothes.'

'You prefer Tara?'

'No babe, I prefer you, but I like cool chicks.'

'I don't know how to be cool.'

'Well to start with, you could change your hair.'

'Like Tara's?'

'Yeah.'

'You'd like me to have long black hair?'

'I think short, spiky black hair would be even cooler.'

'You want me to cut my hair?'

'It would look awesome.'

'What else?'

'Some tats would go down well, and maybe a piercing. I'll buy you some nice stuff to wear.'

'Is that what you want?'

'If you want to come with me to the rock festival, it is.'

*

That was the beginning of Elise's transformation. Janet was distraught when she saw Elise's hair. 'How could you do that to your hair?' she sobbed.

'I'm nineteen. It's my choice.'

'Your father is trying to organise a job for you with Melville and Son. You'll be articled to them. How do you think people in a prestigious city law office will put up with that?'

'You should see the kids at Uni. They all look like this.'

On the day of the festival, David Seymour opened the door. Elise was close behind him.

'Hi, Mr Seymour.'

'You're off to a music festival, I'm told,' his voice cold.

'Yeah, out at Liverpool.'

'I've read about what goes on at those things. You look after her, Richard. If anything happens to Elise, you'll be accountable.'

'This one's well controlled they'll have sniffer dogs. No one can get in with drugs.'

'I'm pleased to hear that.'

Turning on the ignition, he exploded with laughter. 'Your old man's something else! He believed that shit about sniffer dogs. What a silly old coot.'

'You're so wicked,' Elise laughed.

'We'll stop off at my place. I've got something for you.' His flat sat atop a corner convenience store, a few blocks away from the Seymour house. It comprised a bedroom, kitchenette, small sitting room and a tiny bathroom. He handed Elise a wrapped parcel.

'What is it?'

'Open it.'

She pulled at the paper. Inside she found a shiny black two-piece outfit. The top had a plunging neckline and thin straps. The bottom was just a pair of short shorts.

'Like it?' He grinned.

Elise wasn't sure what it was...sleep wear, swim suit?

'What's it for?'

'For today, to wear to the festival, put it on.'

Elise took off her jeans and top.

'Hang on don't go any further, time for a quickie.'

Elise was now on the pill and had lost all fear of pregnancy. She was always anxious to please him and would follow his instructions during their sexual encounters. Today he wanted fellatio. This bothered Elise, it seemed more sinful than normal sex, but if that's what Rick wanted.

*

As she dressed in her new outfit, he pulled a small plastic container from his pocket, took off the cap, and shook a heart shaped pill onto his palm.

'Might as well get ourselves primed, open your mouth.'

'What is it?'

'Ecstasy. It'll make you feel good, the music will be awesome.'

Elise opened her mouth and he popped the pill onto her tongue.

'Good girl. Let's get moving. I've arranged to meet the gang in the car park.'

Tara, Travis, Courtney and Emmet were waiting. Already the temperature was soaring. Tara was wearing a tiny skirt and bra top which displayed her many tattoos. Black, red and green dragons writhed across her shoulders and purple flowers decorated her thighs. Courtney was more conservative. She wore a loose T-shirt and baggy three-quarter pants which covered her chubby legs. Tara greeted them with high-five slaps. 'C'mon, the place is already half full. If we want a decent spot, we'd better get moving.'

'They're not letting in grog,' lamented Travis.

'No probs. We've got our little purple hearts.'

'Love your outfit,' Tara patted Elise's shoulder as they

walked to the gate.

Inside the huge paddock, a stage had been erected. Musicians were already up there, tuning their instruments, and sound technicians were busy testing equipment.

They pushed their way through and settled six rows back from the stage. Courtney pulled a small bottle from her pocket. She took a mouthful of the clear liquid. 'You can have your little purple pills. I'll have vodka any time. '

'Lucky you weren't caught,' Tara sniffed.

'Why do you think I wear baggy pants?'

Hundreds of people were teeming in, and already there was angst amongst the crowd. 'Hey, watch it, man,' Rick yelled as a tall gangly youth knocked him.

The microphone came to life when a heavy man with a shaved head yelled for quiet.

'Welcome fans. Today you're going to hear six of the best heavy metal rock bands in the country.' His voice was drowned out by the loud cheering and squealing. He continued talking but his words died under the noise. He gave up and waved a hand to the first group who were ready to go. He made one last successful shout: 'Let's rock and roll'. The drummer gave a long drum roll which was followed by whistling and shouting from the crowd.

Elise would normally feel totally out of place in this sort of scene, but strangely, she felt part of it. She clapped to the music, stamped her feet and twirled around. The music was awesome!

The festival was out of control almost from the beginning. Numbers had exceeded expectations and there weren't enough security people to handle the crowd. People were getting higher with every performance. Pushing and shoving led to brawling, and the guards had their work cut out. The sun was beating down fiercely, and clouds of dust were rising from the stamping feet of the gyrating dancers.

'Enjoying it, babe?'

'Awesome.'

'Time for a booster, open your mouth, tongue out.' He popped a pill onto her tongue.

Within ten minutes, Elise felt weird. Her head was throbbing and seemed disconnected from her body. It was scary. She felt the crowds closing in, suffocating, frightening. The heat was frying her brain. Suddenly she felt the music was just for her and no one else. She was the star of the show! She stumbled away from him.

'Hey, where are you going?' He tried to follow but was blocked by the hordes. Elise made it to the stage and climbing up, grabbed the microphone from the lead singer. She skipped around the stage, half shouting half singing into the microphone, waving her free arm around. One of the performers grabbed her and pulled the microphone out of her grasp. Now the fans were shouting: *Go chick, Go chick*. All attention was on Elise. She had no microphone but she was dancing erratically. She pulled off her top and waved it around. The sweat on her bare breasts glistened in the sunlight. Two security people climbed on the stage and dragged her off. She was clawing and kicking them. 'I'm the star. I'm the star,' she shouted.

Rick pushed his way across. 'God what's happening?'

'She's your friend?'

'Yeah.'

'Well get her out of here, before she's charged.' He threw Elise's top at him.

Travis helped Rick carry Elise to the car park. She was struggling and shouting all the way: 'I'm the star. My fans want me.' By the time they got to the car, Elise was barely conscious. Her eyes were wide open and staring. 'Elise, can you hear me?' Rick yelled. When there was no response, he grabbed his water bottle from the front seat and poured the warm liquid over her neck and chest. When she didn't respond, he slapped her face. No response.

'You'd better get her to Liverpool hospital. It's not far,' Travis muttered.

'Help me with this.' Together they pulled the top over Elise's head and dragged the shoulder straps over her limp arms. It was like dressing a rag doll.

Within minutes of arrival at the hospital, Elise was whisked away on a wheeled bed. Rick sat stiffly in the small waiting room, which by comparison with the blazing heat outside, was freezing cold. A nurse approached him. 'I'll need the patient's details and yours too. Doctor Halliday will be talking to you shortly.' She handed him a clipboard with an attached form to fill in.

*

'If you want to help your friend, you'll tell me what she's taken.' The doctor spoke cuttingly, glaring daggers at him.

'Ecstasy.' He handed over the packet.

'How many did she consume?'

'Two.'

'At what time?'

'The first was around ten this morning and the second was around one.'

'What other substances was she using?'

'None, just the pills.'

'No alcohol?'

'No.'

'Don't leave here until I say to,' Halliday ordered icily.

His mind was reeling. If Elise died, he'd be an accessory. He'd given her the fucking pills. Twenty minutes went by. It felt like twenty hours. He started pacing the small room.

In spite of the cold, a thin line of sweat formed across his forehead as he watched the doctor approach. 'How is she?'

'She'll pull through,' Halliday glared. 'Where did you get those pills?'

'I don't know where she got them.'

'But they were yours I presumed.'

'No. I was only looking after them for her. She didn't have a pocket in her outfit and asked me to look after them,' he lied.

'How old is Elise?'

'Nineteen.'

'How long has she been using?'

'I think this was her first time.'

'What was she doing when she collapsed?'

'Dancing.'

'Just dancing?'

'Yeah.'

'Leading up to collapse, had Elise displayed any psychotic behaviour?'

'No.'

'You sure?'

'Yeah, she just collapsed.'

The doctor's expression was hard as steel. 'We'll keep her in overnight. Her parents should be informed.'

'They're overseas, I'll look after her.'

'How old are you?'

'Twenty-five,' he lied.

'Give all your contact details and your identification to the nurse before you leave, please.' The doctor's tone was scathing. He didn't believe a word.

'I've already filled in the form,' Rick muttered.

Missing In Red

When he picked her up the following day, Elise was trying hard to appear normal.

'She's not to be left alone today, understand? She should have bed rest and avoid activity...of any sort.' The last three words were delivered with a thundering voice and a glaring eye. The nurse handed him a small packet. 'These tablets are to rehydrate. She's to take two every four hours and drink lots of water in between. At the first sign of any relapse, you are to bring her here without delay.'

They walked in silence to his car. Elise flopped onto the passenger seat.

'What did you tell my parents?'

'They think you're at Tara's.'

'Why would they believe that?'

'Tara did you a real favour. She called your folks and lied her head off, said you were at her place, that you were exhausted after the concert and had fallen asleep and you'd be staying the night. Your father asked for her address but Tara hung up.'

'I don't care what Tara told them. My parents would never accept my not coming home, especially after a rock concert.'

'Here, phone them now. Tell them you're sorry and you'll be home soon.' he handed Elise his mobile phone.

'I can't.'

'It's only eight o'clock. If you don't call now, they'll probably go to the police.'

Tears streamed down her cheeks as she made the call. Janet Seymour answered.

'Elise, oh thank God. Why didn't you come home?'

'We called in at Tara's. We were just watching television. I'd had too much sun, and I fell asleep.'

'And where's Richard?'

'He went home.'

'Are you still at Tara's?'

'Yes. I'll be home in an hour.' She hit the 'end' button and turned to him.

'They'll know something bad happened when they see me.'

'Well, you're just going to have to put on a good act. Have a shower at my place and brighten yourself up. Don't forget to take the stuff the nurse gave us.'

After she showered, Elise dressed in the jeans and shirt she'd started out with yesterday. Was it only yesterday? It seemed like a lifetime ago. She had no memory of anything after the second pill. She looked at herself in the mirror. Her eyes were puffy and strange looking. 'Look at my eyes Rick. They'll know I've taken drugs.'

'Put on your sunglasses.'

'I can't keep my sunglasses on all day.'

'The meds the hospital gave you will have you looking normal quick smart. I'll drop you off at the corner. You can walk, okay?'

'I don't know. Why don't you drive me home?'

'Now that's not thinking, is it? If your folks see me, they'll know your story's a load of shit.'

Although it was less than fifty metres Elise had trouble putting one foot in front of the other. She was shaking by the time she got to the house. Janet opened the door.

'Elise, you had us so worried.'

'Sorry mum. I had heatstroke. It was so hot and there were so many people, all pushing and shoving.' Elise walked past her mother, through the hall to the kitchen. She poured herself a glass of water and drank in long thirsty gulps. Janet stood nearby watching. She waited until Elise had finished drinking and then snatched off her sunglasses. She peered into her face. 'You look terrible. I'm taking you to the doctor.'

'I'm okay, truly mum. I've had medical attention.'

'What sort of medical attention?'

'Soon after we stopped in at Tara's, her friend Tess arrived, unexpectedly. Tess is a senior nurse. She took one look at me and said I'd had heatstroke. She gave me these hydrating tablets, said that was the right treatment for heatstroke. If you take me to the doctor, that's all they'll give you.'

'Let me look.' Janet grabbed the package from Elise and read the label. 'They're from Liverpool hospital.'

'That's where Tess works. She uses them herself when she gets de-hydrated.'

Janet's forehead creased. Elise had never lied to her. She did look as if she'd had too much sun. 'That's still no reason why you didn't come home,' she argued.

'I told you, I fell asleep. The heat had really affected me. Apparently, Tess said I should be left to sleep it off.'

'Right, well you're still not recovered, so bed for you for the rest of the day.'

Elise collapsed into her bed sighing with relief. All the lies had been swallowed.

Rick called the following morning. 'Hi babe, how's it going?'

'I'm fine Rick.'

'Awesome. How did the olds handle it?'

'I surprised myself I told them I'd had heat stroke. Don't know where I got that from, but they believed me.'

'Genius babe.' There was a long pause. 'Elise?'

'Yes Rick.'

'Um.'

'What is it, Rick?'

104

'Just wondering if you'd like a night out at the cycle dome this coming Friday. Some hot bikers are racing on super-hot machines. It'll be mind-splitting. The gang's coming.'

'If you want to go, then so do I,' Elise said.

'I'll call for you Friday at six. You sure the olds won't skin me alive? I'm safe to enter the hallowed halls?'

'You're so funny Rick. No worries, they believed my story.'

Janet appeared at the door. For a horrible moment, Elise thought she might have heard her last comment.

'Who was that?'

'Rick, he wants to take me out Friday night.'

'You may not be well enough.' Janet's face was wearing the strange mask Elise had come to hate. She also hated her mother's phony accent which all started when her father started in politics.

'That's four days away, I'll be perfectly okay.'

'You've still got that sick look in your eyes. Your father has organised an interview with the senior partner of Melville & Son, Wednesday at eleven. Make sure you stay rested and get well. You must make a good impression.'

'Well, if I'm good enough for an interview on Wednesday, I'm certain to be okay for Friday night.'

Janet Seymour shook her head. 'What's happening to you, Elise? You would never have spoken to me like that before you got in with that rough crowd.'

'They're not rough. They're my friends.'

'Well, one thing's certain. Never ask to go to one of those rock concerts ever again. It was all over the Sunday papers, people brawling, getting stoned, carted off to gaol.'

Elise froze. What was in the papers? She felt Rick had been trying to tell her something. Maybe that was it. She called him. 'Rick, did you know the concert was covered in the Sunday papers?'

'Yeah.'

'Anything I should know?'

'What papers do your olds get?'

'The Sun.'

'Not the Tele?'

'No.'

'That's fucking awesome.'

'What was in the Tele?'

'A photo of you, but don't worry. If they do see it, they'll never recognise you in that outfit. Besides, it wasn't a real clear photo, could have been anyone.'

'What was I doing in the photo?'

'Dancing.'

'Just dancing?'

'Yeah,' he lied. There was no way he would tell Elise that the photo on the front page caught her being dragged from the stage, stoned out of her brain, and bare breasted.

'I wish I could remember. It's all a blank.'

*

Janet opened the door to him. 'Elise is still recovering from that disgraceful circus you exposed her to. We expect her home before midnight.' The tone was abrasive and authoritative.

'Sure Mrs S. No probs.'

He lit a cigarette and turned on the ignition. He exhaled a long stream of smoke and asked: 'Are you sure you're not adopted?'

Elise turned to him grinning. 'Of course, I'm sure. Why do you ask?'

'Those parents of yours came from another planet.'

'Dad's okay. Mother has become a bit of a problem.'

'A bit? He smirked.

'She wants to keep me like a little kid, dress like a little kid, behave like a little kid.' Elise sighed heavily. 'I think there's something wrong with her.'

'Like what?'

'She's not normal, whatever normal is.'

'Ditto, I say to that.'

They drove in comfortable silence and Elise said: 'I've never been to a motorcycle event before.'

'It's the best. You see man and beast working together with the skill of the man and the superior mechanics of the cycle... the beast.'

'I didn't know you were into motorcycles.'

'I've lusted after a Harley all my life.'

'What's a Harley?'

'Just the best motorcycle ever been created.'

Elise watched the big bikes speeding around the arena. The smell of fuel, burning rubber, cigarette smoke, human sweat and beer blending with the deafening roar of the cycles, created an atmosphere she didn't like. To make matters worse, Rick hardly spoke to her and laughed and joked with Tara seated on his other side. Elise felt abandoned. When she saw Tara put her hand on his crotch, she stood.

'I've had enough, I want to go home.'

'It's only just starting, sit down,' he growled.

Elise glared at Tara who merely grinned back at her. 'When are you getting your tats, Elise?'

'I'm not sure I want any.'

'I'll take you to my guy, he's brilliant.'

'Yeah, do that Elise, get cool, get some tats.' He didn't take his eyes off the roaring bikes as he spoke.

'What's the matter with you tonight?' she said sitting down.

He peered at her through bloodshot eyes. 'What do you mean by that?'

'You've ignored me all night, hardly said a word. You didn't even ask how I got on with the interview.'

He took her hand. 'Sorry babe. Well, how *did* you get on with the interview?'

Elise smiled widely. 'I'm in!'

'Does that mean lots of money? I don't have to empty my pockets every time we step out?'

'I'll be articled to the firm silly, still a student.'

'They've got to pay you if you're working for them.'

'I get legal experience working there, and they give me time off to attend lectures. The pay is paltry.'

He shrugged and turned his attention back to the screeching bikes.

*

All those memories bring mixed emotions. Rick turns away from the window to answer the phone buzzing on his desk.

CHAPTER 8
November 2021

Melville & Melville takes up the twenty-fourth floor of one of the most prestigious buildings in the city. Ellington is irritated to find the underground car park packed to the rafters. He drives around the cavernous place three times, his patience sorely tested. The squeal of tyres on the well-worn concrete mixed with the smell of petrol fumes adds to his irritation. He's about to abandon the whole exercise when miraculously, a small sedan pulls out.

He checks the directory in the lift foyer and rides to the twenty-fourth floor. The reception area is spacious. Plush cream carpet tones tastefully with leather chairs, and colourful works of art decorate the walls. A circular desk stands in the centre, its gleaming granite countertop and leather-padded front compliment the luxurious decor. An attractive girl sits behind a computer. At Ellington's arrival, she responds with a flash of brilliant white teeth.

Ellington shows his ID. 'I believe Tara Gresham is an employee here?'

'That's right.' The smile beams like a neon light.

'Would I be able to have a word with her?'

'I think she's in her office. Is something wrong?'

'She's not in any trouble. She might be able to help me with my inquiries into a missing person.'

'Oh.' The girl taps into an intercom device. 'Hello Jo, is Tara Gresham there? There's someone here to see her.'

Ellington surveys Tara Gresham as she enters the foyer...a tall twenties-something girl with wide shoulders and narrow hips. Her long black hair, kohl-lined eyes, purple stained lips and black varnished nails create a gothic look that challenges the expensive green shift clinging to her lean, angular frame. She sullenly gazes at Ellington through dark eyes. 'You want to talk to me? I don't think we've met.'

'Detective Sergeant Ellington. Could we sit somewhere quiet?' He shoots a sideways glance at the listening receptionist.

'Sure.' Tara glides off through open double doors and along a corridor. Ellington follows her into a small room. The carpet theme has carried through, and four leather chairs surround a sculptured coffee table. Tara sits and waves a ring laden hand toward the chair opposite her.

'I'm investigating the disappearance of Elise Seymour.' He watches as Tara's expression changes from slightly bored to open eyed concentration.

'Elise, disappeared?'

'You didn't know?'

'How could I? We don't communicate.'

'Think again, Miss Gresham. You left a message on Elise's mobile phone only a few days ago.'

'Now that you mention it, so I did.'

'Your message was concerning Richard Ballantyne. Correct?'

'Yes.'

'Why did you think Elise would know where Ballantyne was?'

She shrugs. 'I don't know, I just thought she might.'

'Have you any idea at all where Elise could be?'

'She could be with Rick'.

'We've spoken with him, and she's not.'

'In that case, I've no idea.' Tara stands, walks to the door, and turns. 'Is that all?'

'Before Richard Ballantyne, you were in a relationship with Travis Lockhart. Correct?'

'What if I was? I'm not anymore, can't stand the creep.'

'Why is that?'

'He tried to make all sorts of trouble. He threatened both me and Rick.'

'When was this?'

'Soon after Rick and I became an item.'

'How did he threaten you?'

'He came around to our apartment yelling and swearing. He accused me of stealing from him.'

'What were you supposed to have stolen?'

Tara rolls her eyes. 'An iPad, a camera, a blender, a whole list of things, he demanded I hand them over.'

'Did you?'

'I told him to fuck off.'

'Did he?'

'He became abusive and threatening. I laughed and pushed him, he pushed me back. That's when Rick stepped in. He punched Travis in the face.' Tara smiles as she recalls the incident. 'Travis hit back. He's such a weed, I don't think Rick even felt it. Rick punched him again and threw him out the door.'

'Did you hear anything after that?'

'I got a letter from a solicitor. I just ignored it.'

'And?'

'Nothing never heard another peep.'

'I'd like to talk with Travis Lockhart. Can you tell me where to find him?'

'He works at the library, here in the city, Circular Quay. Can I go now?'

Ellington walks slowly towards her. 'One more thing, last Thursday morning between the hours of eight and let's say, ten, where were you?'

'You don't think I've got anything to do with Elise Seymour's disappearance?'

'Your message on her phone was threatening, that can't be ignored.'

Tara bites her bottom lip and for the first time seems to lose her sulky bravado.

'Well?' Ellington pushes.

'At eight I would have been sitting in heavy traffic on my way here.'

'And what time did you arrive here?'

'Around eleven.'

'Eleven? Even with our notorious traffic, driving from Summer Hill to the city would take well under an hour.'

'I was halfway here and had to turn back home. I'd left my wallet behind.'

'And that took two and a half hours?'

'The traffic was abominable.'

'If you plan on leaving the city Ms Gresham, I'd appreciate a call.' He hands her his card. 'We might need to talk again.'

He considers taking the train to Circular Quay, but on second thoughts, decides to walk. Although he's lived all his life in Sydney, it's been a long time since he's actually walked the city streets. He makes his way up to Macquarie Street and notes from the signage, the area is still home to some of the most prestigious medical specialists in the country. On his right spreads the middle section of the abundant green belt devoted to the city, which includes Hyde Park, the Domain and the Royal Botanical Gardens. As he approaches Sydney Harbour, Ellington acknowledges that never once has this view failed to take his breath away. It's undoubtedly the sparkling jewel in the City's crown. In his time, he's been to many great cities. He's admired the beauty of Paris, the historical significance of London and the ancient magnificence of Rome, but for a modern city, Sydney beats them all.

The City Library operates in Customs House, a prominent Georgian relic from the mid-nineteenth century. The multi-level building has been added to and altered over the years and now stands in all its grandeur alongside the glittering harbour. An enormous cruise ship is berthed at Circular Quay, and a ferry bound for Manly is just departing. Ellington allows himself the luxury of five minutes to savour his beautiful surroundings. The combined smell of sea water and diesel fuel brings back memories of a ferry trip taken with his grandmother when he was a small boy. He's back on the ferry, listening to his grandmother's soft voice.

'You know Luke when I was a little girl, they had musicians on the ferries, playing music most of the way to Manly. There were violins, a piano and a piano accordion. It was so jolly sailing along with the lovely music. After a few tunes, they would take around a box, and if you liked the music, you would drop in a penny or two.'

'Why don't they still play music gran?'

'That stopped a long time ago Luke. I don't think people today would play music for a few pennies.'

'Did you often ride the ferry gran?'

'My parents often went to Manly by ferry. We even stayed there for summer holidays. One trip I remember clearly. I was about seven and entertaining myself by reading the posters on the ferry walls. There was one poster that puzzled me. I read it to my father...Seven Miles to Manly and

a Thousand Miles from Care. I had never heard of "care". It sounded like a place. Where's care dad? I asked.'

Ellington smiles at the memories of his lovely grandmother. He was so proud of her when she came to grandparents' day in primary school. She was different to the other grandmothers. They all seemed much older than gran with their grey hair, floral dresses and slow walking. Gran's chestnut-coloured hair was fashionably cut, and she wore tailored jeans and smart tops. In summer, she painted her toenails bright pink. As a kid, he spent a lot of time with gran. Both his parents worked, which meant he was with her every school holiday. He especially loved the summer breaks when she would take him to the beach. The winter holidays were good too. They would cuddle up on the lounge and watch old time movies, mostly from the fifties. *'That period was my heyday,'* gran would say as she recalled her teenage years.

One holiday she taught him to dance. They twirled around the lounge room to the music of the fifties. Other times she would bring out her photo albums. He especially loved looking through the ones when gran was a pretty teenager in beautiful frocks, exotic creations with tiny waists and flaring skirts, just like those Elise Seymour wore. The thought jolts him back to the present. He takes one last look at the world's most beautiful harbour and its magnificent Opera House, before walking towards Customs House.

Ellington enters the pleasantly cool City Library. The ground floor appears to be a reading room which has been set up with numerous comfortable chairs, most of which are occupied. The eerie quietness is broken by an occasional cough or rustling of pages. A sign indicates two upper floors. As no one seems in attendance on the ground level, Ellington climbs the stairs.

At the lending desk, three librarians are attending to

customers. He approaches a fourth girl stacking books.

'I'm looking for Travis Lockhart, can you help me?'

'Travis? I think you'll find him sorting books in the large-print section. Go down the fourth aisle, right to the end, you should find him there.'

'Thanks.' Ellington follows the directions and is soon assessing the slight, red headed young man pushing books around a half-packed shelf. 'Travis Lockhart?'

The man jumps slightly at the sudden intrusion into his deep concentration. He frowns at Ellington. 'Yes?'

Ellington shows his ID. 'Detective Ellington, I'm investigating the recent disappearance of Elise Seymour.'

'Elise? Missing?'

'You didn't know?'

'No, I didn't.'

'She went missing early Thursday. I understand up until a year ago, you were socially connected?'

'We were in the same group for a few years. She wasn't my girlfriend or anything like that.'

'Have you seen or heard from her in the past few weeks?'

'No, I haven't seen Elise in nearly a year.'

'You wouldn't have any idea at all where she might be?'

'No.'

'Have you been in contact at all with Tara Gresham?'

'No thanks, she turned out to be a right piece of goods.'

'Meaning?'

'She stole from me. I lent her thirty thousand dollars, she never paid it back.'

'I spoke to Tara Gresham earlier today. She told me about the argument, didn't mention money said it was just goods.'

'That fits. She *did* take goods, an iPad, a camera, you

name it. I would have let that go, but thirty thousand bucks? no way.'

'That's a lot of money.'

'And I intend getting it back.' Travis angrily slams a book onto the shelf before speaking again. 'She bought Elise Seymour's car with most of it.'

'Have you seen Richard Ballantyne in recent weeks?'

'I don't communicate with him either, he's a total prick. The last time I saw him was the night I went around there demanding my money, that was months ago.'

'There was another couple in the group, I understand.'

'Yes, Courtney and Emmet. They went overseas just after the group broke up. They're staying in England.'

'Where were you on Thursday morning last week?'

'That was the day I drove up to Lauraville to spend a couple of days with my parents.'

'Took some time off work?'

'My mother is ill. I went on compassionate leave.'

Ellington hands Travis Lockhart his card. 'If you think of anything that might help, call me.'

*

Back at the station, Ellington checks his fax. With a whistle of satisfaction, he recovers fifty diary pages sent by Doug Barnes. He examines the deciphered coding, most of the early part focuses on Elise's unhappiness and her dislike of her mother. One entry grabs his attention.

September 18: *The church people are my alibis. I don't expect this will last forever. But Maude Tingwell is useful for Tuesday and Friday nights. Gregory is besotted, and although he repulses me, he needs me. If it wasn't for me, the entire church would crumble, and I can't have that.*

Ellington presses his lips together and wrinkling his brow, reads on. Again, the entries centre on the difficulties

Elise was having with her parents and her boring life at the pharmacy. There are occasional references to Ballantyne, Allenby and Brown.

September 30: I watch him pass the shop every morning and without fail, my heart misses a beat. He never looks in.

November 5: I have decided to stop visiting Gregory. He knows I'm not interested but he keeps trying. I'll give it until Christmas, and then...finished. The situation is getting out of hand.

November 9: Nathan actually propositioned me today, asked me if I would go back to his house after closing up. He came straight out and said he'd fallen in love with me and was desperate to have it off with me. Well, he didn't exactly use those words. I think he said something tacky like wanting to know me more intimately. I put on the little girl act, said my parents were expecting me home for dinner and I thought it best if we kept our relationship on a formal business level. He looked like a fish out of water, gulping.

Blotches on the page of the next entry suggest to Ellington that Elise was crying as she wrote.

November 13: Tonight, he raped me. I don't know what to do. If I tell, so many people will be affected. I have to keep silent.

Ellington sits back, and rubs his hand across his eyes. Who raped her? Was it Allenby or Brown? They were both after her.

He continues reading: *I'd just showered off his filth when out of the blue Tara phoned. She sounded desperate and demented. Rick's left her and she thinks he's back with me. She demanded I tell her where he is. This is what I've been dreaming of for so long. He's coming back. Oh, heavenly bliss, my heart is jumping. I told her I didn't wish to discuss*

Rick with her and closed off. She called back I didn't answer. She left a nasty text. I've been looking at my phone all night, waiting for him to ring. It's now eleven and he hasn't called. Maybe he's planning to see me tomorrow, I can't wait.

The next entry is her last. It was written the night before she disappeared:

November 14: He's left Tara but he's not interested in me. I am crucified, I am drowning in pain. How can people be so cruel? I've done nothing to deserve this. I know now what I must do.

Ellington looks up and glancing across the room meets the eyes of Sarah Bradley. He feels a pang of guilt as he hasn't included her in any of the afternoon's work. He wanders over. 'I've made some headway in the Seymour case, fancy a drink?'

Sarah glances at her watch. It's nearly five and she could definitely do with a drink. 'Okay.'

They head for the local pub which has served as the Station's watering hole for many decades. Sarah leads them to a small booth away from most of the noisy chatter.

'What'll it be?' asks Ellington.

'White wine, thanks.'

Ellington returns with the drinks and slides in beside Sarah. She clinks her glass against his. 'Cheers.'

'The diary's been decoded. Elise recorded she'd recently been raped.'

Sarah whistles softly, 'who?'

'She doesn't say, but it has to be either the pastor or the chemist.' Ellington takes a swig of his beer. 'I interviewed Tara Gresham today.'

'What did *she* have to say?'

'She doesn't appear to have an alibi for her movements last Thursday morning, and denies having any contact with

Elise, other than the recent phone call.'

'You think she could be involved in Elise's disappearance?'

'She has a motive, and she left a threatening message.'

'What she like?'

'Not the type I'd take home to meet mother.'

'Oh?'

'She's flamboyant, confident, creepy.'

'Creepy?'

'Looks like a bloody vampire.' He takes another mouthful of beer and peers thoughtfully beyond Sarah. His eyes fix on a half-dead blowfly crawling up the wall. He watches it as he speaks. 'I also saw the ex-boyfriend, Travis Lockhart.'

'You *did g*et around today. What did *he* have to say?'

'Talked about the argument he'd had with Tara. Apparently, he'd lent her a lot of money and never got it back. I'd say there was a lot of bitterness there.'

Sarah takes a sip of wine and says wistfully, 'She's only been missing six days yet it feels like six months.'

'Tomorrow I'm driving to Canberra to talk with the lobbyist who threatened Seymour. Want to come?' As he speaks, the destroyed fly gives up the ghost and free falls into Sarah's handbag.

CHAPTER 9

It's a magnificent late spring morning. The Canberra streets and gardens are alive with brilliant colours. Stuart Partridge's house is double-storied and set on a wide block. Ellington checks his watch. Their appointment is for eleven and it's now one minute before.

Partridge is a very overweight man with thinning hair framing a ruddy, jowly face. He is casually dressed in grey slacks, a checked shirt and a grey unbuttoned cardigan.

'Come through. I'm afraid I've another appointment at eleven-thirty so hope this won't take long.' They follow him through a short hall. Partridge walks slowly, adopting the careful dainty walk often used by morbidly obese people.

They enter a sunny sitting room which is further brightened by yellow cushions and curtains. Partridge indicates a cane sofa and sits on an opposite chair.

'Now, how can I help you?'

'You are acquainted with David Seymour?'

'I am.'

'Mr Seymour's daughter disappeared last Thursday morning, most uncharacteristic. Foul play has been suggested and we can't deny that possibility.'

'What's that got to do with me?'

120

'We understand that you made a threat to Mr Seymour the last time you were with him.' Ellington briefly consults his notebook and with raised eyebrows says, 'September fifteenth.'

'Threat? I did no such thing. You'd better tell me what he said.'

'Seymour was uncertain of the exact words but said it involved your lobby for a *Yes* vote in the Bill concerning the State Police. You said he would be sorry if he didn't support the Bill.'

'Rubbish. If I went around threatening people, I'd be out of a job in two shakes.'

'What *did* you say, Mr Partridge, when you called on David Seymour?' Sarah's voice is low and officious.

'All I said was: The party needs your vote. This is a very important Bill and you should support it. That's all'.

'You didn't use any threatening language?'

'None at all.'

'Have you anything at all you can tell us that might assist us in finding this missing girl?'

Partridge stands. 'Sorry, now if we're finished?' He extends his arm towards the door. Ellington and Sarah take the hint.

The midday heat has settled on the city, and the car is boiling hot. Sarah removes her hat and flicks a hand across her fringe. 'A long way to come to hear nothing.'

Ellington starts the car and turns on the air conditioning. 'Had to be done. I've made an appointment with the independent supporting the Bill. I'm not expecting anything to come of that either, but as we're here...'

Five minutes later they are in the family room of Ian Wood. Ellington is surprised that someone so young could have a seat in Parliament. The man looks no more than twenty-five. He greets them with an engaging smile. His wife, a pretty Asian girl offers them coffee.

'Thanks for seeing us Mr Wood.'

'Ian', the man corrects.

Ellington smiles and nods, 'you probably don't know about the disappearance of David Seymour's daughter.'

'I do actually. We saw it on the television, terrible business.'

The coffee arrives with milk, sugar and biscuits. Mrs Wood sits next to her husband. He places a protective arm around her shoulder and juggles his coffee with his free hand.

'How well do you know David Seymour, Ian?'

'We've never mixed socially.'

'Is there anything at all you could tell us that might throw some light on his daughter's disappearance?'

'Do you think she might have been kidnapped?' Wood's voice shows concern.

'It's possible.' Ellington stretches his neck, and fixes Wood with probing eyes. 'How do you get on with David Seymour?'

Wood frowns. 'Okay, but as I said, we are only involved in the business of the Parliament.'

'You are both Independents. Do you not sometimes meet up to compare notes?'

'No. Independent means just that, independent. We follow our own conscience.'

'What about the Bill you and Seymour are divided on, the Bill currently being debated about the State Police?'

'He'll vote his way and I'll vote mine, simple as that.'

'Has Stuart Partridge approached you?'

'Yes. That's his job.'

'Seymour accuses Stuart Partridge of threatening him for not supporting the Bill. Does that surprise you?'

'It does. I've never known Stuart to threaten anyone.'
*

Ellington pulls into a roadside cafe, an open-air establishment with long wooden tables and benches. Grape vines wind their way through an overhead trellis and soft Greek music plays in the background. Sarah studies the menu. 'I'll have the Greek salad and a tomato juice.' The waiter approaches, a heavy-set man with a thick black moustache and a crop of wavy black hair. Surprisingly, he speaks with an Australian accent. 'What'll it be, guys?'

'The Greek salad and tomato juice for the lady and the moussaka and a light beer for me.'

Sarah stares out to the adjoining paddock. Horses are grazing and the smell of smoke mingled with freshly mown grass drifts in. A rooster crows in the distance and a young magpie struts up to the table. She feels a wave of insouciance envelop her, something she hasn't felt in a long time. Their meals come and they eat in silence.

After a while, Sarah breaks the silence. 'What made you become a policeman?'

Ellington smiles. 'It wasn't what I had in mind, but circumstances prevailed.'

'Circumstances?'

'My father was a tradesman, good at his job, but the pay wasn't great. Yet he paid off the mortgage and gave us a good life. Mum took on a part time job so that my sister and I could go to private schools. When dad died at fifty, I was in year twelve and my sister was in year three. I had decided that I wanted to be a forensic scientist. I loved science. But with dad gone, university now was out of the question.'

'How sad.'

'Well, I had to look elsewhere. Police work seemed the closest thing to forensic science, and I figured that as an adult student I could eventually put myself through uni.'

'Are you still thinking of doing that?'

'It's a bit late now. I somehow seem to have settled into the job.'

'You've lost the urge?'

'Seems that way' He takes a sip of his beer. 'What about you? Why did you join the Force?'

'Since I was little, I've wanted to be a police girl.'

Ellington nods slowly and finishes his beer. 'Like some coffee?'

'I don't think so.'

'Okay, then let's hit the road.'

The traffic moves well and the sun is starting to dip down.

'We might be home before dark,' he says.

'What's on the agenda for tomorrow, Luke?'

Ellington shifts slightly in his seat. Hearing a female voice pronounce his name like that, stirs memories.

'It's back to the church people. Elise was using one of them to give her an alibi when she visited Allenby. I'll need to talk with them all again.'

The trip home is quietly comfortable. Sarah looks sideways at Ellington. She likes the set of his jaw and admires the strong tanned hands on the steering wheel. She notes the absence of a wedding ring. She rests her head back and closes her eyes.

Her mind travels back to when she first decided to join the Force. She was eleven years old and had been watching a crime series on television. The stars of the show were two female detectives. 'That's what I want to be,' she excitedly told her parents. They smiled indulgently and hoped she would grow out of the weird notion. She never did. On the day she completed her Higher School Certificate she started making inquiries.

Now seven years in the Force she has already been promoted to Senior Constable. With her promotion came a change of location. Moving from Sydney's outer west to the city, was a refreshing change. Her new location is busy and meaningful, no longer is she focusing on petty theft, domestic violence and drunken brawls. Here is the real stuff, major crime. Most of her colleagues are friendly, but from day one, Detective Sergeant Ellington has had her mesmerised. He seemed different from the others, refined, efficient and quietly authoritative. He was unaware that Sarah watched him a lot, but one day she was caught looking. It was the day they started on the Seymour case. Inspector Bellamy was sitting near Ellington's desk. They were going through a file when suddenly they both turned and looked straight at her. She turned back to her computer with flaming heat spreading over her cheeks, and started typing frantically.

She glances again at Ellington. He seems deep in thought.

'You married?' She surprises herself with the blurted question.

'Nope.'

'Got a girlfriend?'

'Nope.'

'How come?'

I'm not gay if that's what you're angling for.'

Silence reigns for a few minutes.

'For that matter, are you married, constable?'

'No and I don't have a boyfriend and I'm not gay.'

That's another thing we have in common.'

'What else is there?'

Ellington tries to suppress his grin. 'We are both officers of the law.'

'How could I forget?'

Sarah's questions were logical and he muses: *Why at the age of thirty-two do I not have a wife, kids, a house, a mortgage?* He glances sideways at Sarah. Her eyes are closed and a small smile plays around her mouth. She's probably asleep, he thinks.

Ellington allows his musing to go a step further, back all those years ago to when he first broke up with Nikki.

He was lonely for a while but there were plenty of single mates to knock around with. He surfed on Sundays and went to the football on Saturdays. He liked his job and was working hard toward promotion.

A cop was killed in the line of duty and a memorial service was organised. His station was part of the huge contingent of police attending. It was here he spotted Zac Histon, a good mate from the Academy. They'd lost touch after graduation… something Ellington had often regretted.

'Hey mate, how's it going?'

Zac's expression was one of genuine pleasure. 'Duke!'

They vigorously shook hands. 'We gotta get together for a drink.'

'Name it mate. I'll be there.'

'Where you stationed?'

'Sutherland.'

'Cool, I'm at Hurstville.'

They met at a pub midway between both areas. Catching up was easy, the friendship was still there, free and spontaneous. Zac had a live-in girlfriend and it sounded serious.

'Going away for Christmas Duke?'

'Nope, thinking of taking some time off mid-year instead, skiing.'

'Doing anything New Year's Eve?'

'Nothing organised, yet.'
'We're throwing a party, come along and meet Chrissie.'

*

Ellington hated party small talk and deliberately arrived late. The house was a semi-detached in Rockdale. The roof was flashing Christmas lights, and loud music was blaring from the front living room. The night was warm and balmy. People were in the front garden, the back garden and inside the house. He was surprised at the numbers. Zac hadn't said it was going to be a big party.

Zac accepted the bottle of scotch and grabbed his arm. He pulled him towards a short, dark-haired girl juggling an overloaded tray of savouries. 'Hey Duke, meet the beautiful Chrissie.'

Chrissie smiled. 'Glad you could come, Duke, I've heard a lot about you.'

'That's a worry,' he grinned.

'And here's my sister Angie,' said Zac.

Ellington turned to face a beautiful woman. Five-inch heels brought her grey-green eyes level with his. Her aqua outfit with a plunging neckline and bare midriff revealed gleaming tanned skin. She flashed an incredibly white smile as they shook hands.

The rapport was immediate. The fact that Angela was seven years his senior, was of no consequence to either of them. He admired her sophistication and intelligence and adored her wicked sense of humour. He was hooked.

Within six weeks, she had moved into his apartment. Unlike Nikki, Angela had a strong work ethic. She was employed by a prominent advertising agency and was a senior executive. She had her own clients who paid dearly for her bright ideas and clever jingles, and her salary almost doubled his. The job frequently took her interstate for two, sometimes three days at a time. Even when home, she would often be entertaining clients at city restaurants.

The relationship also had to cope with his shifts, some of which started at midnight and saw him coming home just as Angela was leaving. But for all that, the relationship was dynamic and satisfying.

As time went by, things started changing. He often felt belittled by her fierce independence and superior attitude, but he had to reluctantly remind himself that she was a high-flying executive and he was just a cop. These thoughts encouraged extra effort toward his first promotion.

While Angela's client dinners increased in frequency their romantic encounters were decreasing. Angela seemed constantly pre-occupied.

One morning while she was in the shower, her mobile went off. Ellington answered and the caller cut out. Angela came out with a towel wrapped around her waist, her wet hair smelling of apple blossom. 'That my phone?'

'They hung up.'

'Oh?' She frowned. 'That's been happening a lot lately to everyone. We think it's those people overseas trying to sell stuff. They call, pretending they're employed by local companies.'

'It doesn't happen to me,' he muttered.

They rarely breakfasted together, but one Friday morning in early March was an exception. 'You've got the midnight shift, right?' she asked draining her coffee.

'Yeah, and you've got a client dinner, right?'

She nodded and headed out.

Almost immediately, his phone went off. It was his chief. 'Ellington, I want you to change your shift. Can you start midday?'

'No problem.'

He did his shift, was home at eight, cooked some chops, poured a beer and settled down to a night of television. He decided he'd stay up for Angela, and give her a surprise, she should be home by midnight. He fell asleep in front of the television. When he woke, the clock showed ten after midnight. Angela was still out and he went to bed.

He woke at six and there was no sign of Angela. She breezed in at seven, her face collapsed when she saw him sitting there.

'Must have been a good night,' he rasped.

'How come you're not at work?'

'Big surprise!' he sneered. 'How come you didn't come home?'

'I stayed at Debbie's.'

'And who is Debbie?'

'One of the girls who often comes to client dinners, we got friendly.'

'You've never mentioned her before.'

'She doesn't work with us, she freelances.' Angela sighs. 'I drank too much, and the random breath guys were all over the place. I couldn't risk it. I was going to call for a cab when Debbie suggested I stay at her place. She's not far from the restaurant, she drove me back there this morning for my car.' Suddenly Angela lost her defensive attitude. 'Hell, is this an inquisition? For God's sake!' she stormed out of the room. He admitted to himself it could all be true and decided not to carry it further.

The following Sunday they woke to a magnificent day. Although autumn, the weather was magic, perfect for the beach. He had his board and Angela had her book. He was paddling towards the shore when he saw her talking with a tall grey-headed man. As he picked up his board, he watched them walk to the kiosk.

He waited on the sand for Angela to return. 'Who was that?'

'One of our clients, Paul Cunningham.'

'Did you buy him coffee?'

She laughed. 'No silly, he bought *me* coffee.'

'When's the next client dinner?'

'Tuesday.'

'Where are you going?'

'Marcos in the city.'

'Many going?'

'At least eight.'

'Cunningham?'

'I think so.'

'Who actually pays for these dos?'

'I've told you, the company. Clive Benning picks up the tab and the company pays.'

On Monday, he phoned Marcos. 'I'm checking a booking for tomorrow evening. It should be in the name of either Clive Benning or maybe Dulwich Advertising. I think it's for around eight people. I'm hoping to add my name.'

'Just a moment sir, I'll check the reservations book.' After a small interval, the waiter spoke again: 'I'm afraid there's no booking for tomorrow night in either of those names. In fact, the only large booking we have is for a group of young women. All the other bookings are for twos and fours.'

'Thanks, I'm sorry to have bothered you.' Before leaving that day, he borrowed a tracking device from the station. While Angela was sleeping, he fixed it to her car.

When he finished his shift at six, he checked the tracking device. Angela's car was still stationary. He drove the short distance to her office and parked at a meter two streets away. The traffic was dense and chaotic. At six-thirty, the small screen showed Angela's car in motion. It was only minutes before he realised tailing without the device would have been impossible. He had lost sight of her already.

The device tracked Angela heading over the harbour bridge and then travelling north, up the Pacific Highway. The car eventually left the highway at Pymble, and after travelling a short distance, came to a standstill. When he turned into the street, he saw Angela's car parked outside a huge house. He parked on the opposite side several houses further down. Darkness was falling and he felt relatively secure under its cover. He watched the house, lights were on, upstairs and down. The well-manicured garden was illuminated by light coming from the spaced lamp posts.

After thirty minutes a late model Mercedes rolled down the circular drive and out through the open double wrought iron gates. As it passed, he could see two people in the front. Now he had to rely on his own tailing expertise. As they were well out of the city, and traffic was relatively light, following them wasn't difficult. The Mercedes reached the highway and after a short distance, parked outside a small restaurant. Ellington drove past, did a U-turn at the end of the street, and parked opposite. He watched as the couple passed under the bright entrance light and disappeared inside. He waited five minutes and then walked across the road. The glass frontage of the restaurant allowed him a good look inside. He cautiously took a peek, turning his head and keeping his body out of view. This was a risk, if Angela happened to be looking in his direction, he would be sprung, but he was lucky. She was staring intently into the face of the man sitting opposite her, the same man he had seen at the beach. Ellington's jaw clenched as Cunningham reached across the table and took Angela's hand. Ellington had seen enough. He felt both anger and sorrow, but by the time he was home, he had made his decision.

She arrived home at one-thirty. He feigned sleep.

'So how was Marcos last night?' He casually asked the next morning.

'We didn't end up going to Marcos. Clive cancelled, said he thought the Thai place at Crows Nest was a better deal.'

'So, you went to Crows Nest?'

'Yeah,' she finished her coffee. 'Gotta get moving, got a big day ahead.' She picked up her bag and headed towards the door.

'Why are you cheating on me?'

She turned back to him her eyes wide. 'Sorry?'

'You heard. Why are you lying? I know where you were last night and it wasn't with a group of eight and it wasn't at Crows Nest. Sit down.' His voice was harsh and commanding.

Angela returned slowly to her seat. She plonked her Gucci bag on the table and spoke softly. 'What do you want to know?'

'Not everything. I don't really want to know everything, like how long all this has been going on, etcetera, but I would like to know why.'

'I love you, Luke.'

'No, you don't. I doubt if you even love that guy you were with. I think the only person you love, is yourself. Now tell me why.'

'I honestly don't know why. I get lonely when you're on those funny shifts. I suppose that's got something to do with it.'

'Oh? And what about me when you go on your funny interstate trips and have your funny client dinners? I get lonely too, but I don't go around shagging my female colleagues or anyone else for that matter.'

'Can you forgive me? I won't do it again.'

'I can forgive you Angela, but I can never trust you. Without trust, there's nothing. I want you to leave.'

'Where? You know what the rental market is.'

'I don't really care. You can go and shack up with Debbie, that is if there really is a Debbie.'

'Give me time to find something.'

'I'll give you a week. After that, if you're not out, your clothes will be decorating the street.'

During the following week, he totally avoided Angela. She left on the sixth day.

Zac phoned a few weeks later and they arranged to meet for a drink.

'It's not the first time she's done that. I didn't think it would happen again.'

Ellington raised his eyebrows with an unspoken question.

'He was a really nice guy, she hoodwinked him too,' Zac sighed.

'Why?'

'She's thirty-something, never married. I think she's trying to prove she's still attractive and seductive.'

'You could've warned me.'

'Sorry mate, I just didn't think she'd do it to you.'

*

Ellington returns to the present and looks sideways at Sarah. The smile has gone and now there's a slight furrow between her closed eyes. He doesn't notice the tiny tear trickling down her cheek.

They are now passing through the Southern Highlands. His thoughts travel to Carly who came more than a year after Angela. She was a teller at the local bank and the attraction was immediate. They always enjoyed a bit of banter when he called in to withdraw cash, and as time went on, he found himself dropping in more often than necessary.

'You know you can save time by going to an ATM,' she grinned.

'But then I'd miss out on seeing you.'

Eventually, he asked her out to dinner. Carly was the antithesis of Angela. While Angie was self-confident and sophisticated, Carly was quiet and shy. However, she loved sex, and it wasn't long before she was a regular sharer of his king bed. It was a peaceful relationship until Carly started talking about marriage and babies.

'I'm not ready for kids,' he protested.

'My time's running out.'

'You're only twenty-five, what's the rush?'

'My biological clock, that's what. The younger you are, the healthier your kids will be.'

The argument became a daily one, and finally he ended the relationship. He missed Carly and the good sex and her wonderful cooking, but couldn't bear the thought of babies and all the strife that probably went with them.

Sarah shifts in her seat and her eyelids flutter. She sighs deeply and Ellington wonders what she's dreaming about. His mind settles on the most traumatic of his relationships...Rachel. He met her four years ago at a colleague's birthday party. He can almost feel the humidity as he remembers the close, hot night. The small apartment was coping badly with the sixty or more guests who were jammed together like sardines. The deafening dance music made conversation impossible and he immediately regretted coming. He grabbed a beer and made his way out to the deck. Here he found her, leaning on the balustrade gazing out at the night sky. She wore a strapless black dress that clung to her slender, shapely body. Shining auburn hair tumbled over her shoulders.

'This is better,' he said. She looked at him with amazing green eyes and smiled. 'Too noisy and too crowded for my liking,' she took a sip of her drink.

He took her home and that was the beginning of an exciting affair.

But over time, the excitement took a turn and became more of an explosion. At first, he wasn't particularly concerned over Rachel's frequent bouts of intoxication. He didn't think she was drinking heavily, and just assumed because of her slight frame, she was easily affected by grog, but more and more frequently, when they were out, she would do something silly, say something stupid, or worst of all, completely pass out.

And then he started finding the bottles, some empty, some half full, all hidden in the most amazing places. He asked her about them. She avoided the question, and it all hung uneasily in the air. There were days when she cancelled work and stayed in bed, ate nothing and slept.

It came to a head a few weeks after the 'hidden bottles' incident. They were at a party. Rachel was at the bar pouring a drink, she was already unsteady and slurring her words. He took the glass from her. 'You've had enough.'

'Don't you tell me what to do,' she picked up a glass and poured another.

'I'm leaving and you're coming with me.'

She threw the drink in his face and toppled over at the same time. He left the party with Rachel in his arms, totally unconscious.

'Why do you get so plastered?' he asked the next morning.

'What happened?'

'You don't remember?'

'The last thing I remember was talking with Danni.'

He remembered seeing Rachel talking with Danni. That was an hour before the drinking episode. She had lost all memory of that last hour.

'You've lost at least an hour of the party. You don't remember throwing your drink in my face?'

Rachel's eyes filled with tears. 'Oh Luke, please tell me you're joking. I couldn't do that.'

'You did. Rachel, you need help, I think you're an alcoholic. There's an AA place in the next suburb I want you to join. Here's the number.' He handed her a slip of paper.

'I'm not sitting with a crowd of smelly old drunks. You can't ask me to.'

'If you don't, you'll end up a smelly old drunk yourself. I'm not asking, I'm telling. If you don't, we're through.'

Rachel went three times but the drinking continued. He threw out the bottles but Rachel would just go out and buy more. Sometimes she would sit in the local tavern and drink alone.

'You're not making an effort.'

'There are twenty people at AA and only two have beaten the piss. The rest of us are still drinking the same as always, and we have to listen to those two braggers preach and sermonise until we could kill them. It's just not working.'

He made an appointment for her to see a medical hypnotist. That too failed.

Living with Rachel was now a nightmare. He couldn't kick her out, she was sick. He contacted her mother.

'I can't have her here,' she moaned.

'She's your daughter,' he yelled.

'I've got to think of my husband.'

'He's her father.'

'No, he's not, her father died twenty years ago. Mark's her stepfather, he won't have her here.'

He took Rachel aside. 'Rachel, I want you to go over to your mother's. You can't stay here.'

'I won't go there. He's my problem, he's why I drink.'

'What happened?'

'He abused me when I was ten, he's an animal.'

'Did you report it?'

'I told mum. She refused to believe me. She's as bad as him.'

Rachel lost her job and was now home constantly, except when she visited the tavern. Her savings were running out and Ellington had to make sure his money was always in his pocket in the daytime and under his pillow when he slept.

One day he came home and she was gone. She had left a note saying she was going to Tasmania with a friend. He had no idea who the friend was, and although concerned, was enormously relieved.

CHAPTER 10

All the reminiscing has occupied his mind, and Ellington is surprised to see they are approaching southern Sydney.

Sarah opens her eyes. 'Where are we?'

'Not far now.'

Sarah has been reminiscing too, remembering her childhood and the caring parents who had conceived her in their teens.

Sally and Dean grew up quickly when the baby arrived and were well adjusted and responsible. They sent Sarah to a local convent to be educated, nothing fancy, just a simple parochial convent in Sydney's outer west where parents paid if they could. If not, no questions were asked and no one knew. Her parents paid not only the modest school fees but enrolled her in art classes on the weekend. Throughout her school years, she was an intelligent and enthusiastic student and scored a pass in her Higher School Certificate which opened the door to university. But Sarah's plans did not include university. At the end of year twelve, she announced her intentions: she would enter the police force. Her fellow students were astounded at her choice. Even her best friend Belle didn't understand, and argued: 'It's ironic, with your marks you could do anything, but you're choosing to be a cop.

I so wanted to be a vet, but my marks weren't good enough. So now I've got to go for my second choice, I'll be a chef.' Sarah didn't expect Belle to understand, nor did she want to wreck her dreams. She could have said: *Forget that, Belle. With all these TV kitchen shows, the world and his wife want to be a chef. Finding an apprenticeship will be like finding the pot of gold. Maybe you should repeat the year, try for a better result, and do what you really want.* She decided to mind her own business and said nothing.

She knew the police academy would be tough going. She'd heard the stories of misogyny and bullying, but she settled in well, and her quiet demeanour and aloofness seemed to deter victimisation.

Another girl wasn't so lucky. Lana was gullible, naive and a prime target for her tormentors. Sarah's unit was next door to Lana's, and as a result, Sarah was always the first to know when the girl found spiders in her bed sheets, cockroaches in her food, or stones in her shoes. It pained her to see how Lana suffered. It came to a head late one afternoon when Lana came rushing down the hallway screaming. Sarah followed her into her unit, and was appalled to see the hysterical girl's face and head covered in excrement.

'Who did it, Lana?'

The girl just shook her head and stumbled to the shower. Fully dressed, she stayed under the steaming water until Sarah finally came in and turned it off.

Here, have this.' She handed Lana a cup of coffee and sat next to her on the bed. Lana accepted it with two shaking hands. She was wearing Sarah's bathrobe and slippers, her wet hair clung around her face in long straggly wads.

'We've got to stop this, Lana. If you don't complain, I will. Do you have any idea who they are?'

'I think it's Dane Bugden and his crowd, but I'm not positive.'

'Why do you think it's them?'

'Bugden always seems to be around when something happens, grinning stupidly.'

'I'll speak to the captain.'

'No point, Sarah. I'm quitting.'

'You can't let them wreck your career.'

Lana laughed her voice laden with cynicism. 'What career? It was never my idea to join the Force. It was my father's...the old family tradition, great-grandfather, grandfather, father. But dad didn't have a son, did he? Well, the daughter had to do. Now I've got a real excuse to leave. I can't wait to get out.'

'I am still going to complain.'

Her appointment was on the day after Lana left the Academy. The captain listened but quickly dismissed the complaint arbitrarily. 'If you can't positively name the people, then I'm afraid we can't take the complaint any further.'

'The Force has lost a future officer because of what these people are doing. There could be more resignations,' she pleaded.

'That will do, student Bradley. Dismissed.'

She didn't know how or why, but word quickly spread about her complaint. She worried that now she would become the butt of the tormenting. She remembered what they'd done to Lana and always checked her hat and shoes.

Summer just didn't seem to end. It was well into March and still, the weather was hot and humid. The fan in her room was broken and the heat was unbearable. She swiped her ID card at the exit and walked towards the park on the outskirts of town. There was a full moon and the soft balmy breeze wrapped itself around her. The smell of wild jasmine filled the air and for the first time in ages, Sarah had a feeling of contentment. The park by day was a lovely place, home to masses of native bush and full of birdsong. By night it was dark and eerie. She decided against walking further and headed back to the street. A pair of high-beam headlights showered her in bright yellow light.

Male voices shouted: 'You lookin' for it, babe? Well, we're all hot and ready for you.' She was momentarily blinded by the light and stood transfixed for a few seconds. At the sound of a car door slamming and running footsteps approaching, she ran back to the park and into the surrounding bush. She could hear her pursuers' voices, swearing, and cursing. They were gaining and she had to hide. A massive oleander tree with branches spreading to the ground offered refuge. She could now see their shapes, there were four of them. She could smell the alcohol and hear their heavy breathing as they stood in the nearby clearing.

'Where is she?' one yelled.

'Can't be far off.'

She stood like a statue. One rustle of the leaves would give her away. They were so close she could almost reach out and touch them.

'Reckon she's from the Cad?'

'Didn't get a good look at her.'

'Saw her legs though.' A shrill wolf whistle split the air.

They finally moved away. When she heard their car rev up, she left her refuge and avoiding the main road, took the long way 'home' through back streets.

It was nearly midnight when she crawled into bed and pulled the covers over her head. Almost immediately, she felt something cold move onto her leg. She catapulted out of bed and turned on the light. Coiled around her left leg was a long thin snake. A scream choked in her throat as she shook the leg violently. The thing clung on. The adrenalin was pumping through her body and her skin was crawling with fear and repulsion. 'It's only a tree snake, he won't hurt,' she whispered. She bent down and using her thumb and forefinger, took hold of the snake near its head. She then threw it into her duffel bag, pulled the drawstring closed and dropped the bag into a suitcase.

The next morning, she released the snake into the bush. She was determined to find out who was responsible and casually made inquiries about Dane Bugden. She had never spoken with him but knew him by sight, a fellow with a squat build and a head shaped like a bullet. His closely cropped snow-white hair matched his eyebrows and eyelashes. His thick lips were almost red. She caught him watching her, on parade, at pistol practice, in the gym and even in the dining room. She returned his stare with insolence and equal coldness.

It was in the dining room where she found her answer. She heard the voice directly behind her in the queue, a gruff, whining voice. 'Squealers get shit,' was all he said but it was enough for her to know the voice belonged to one of the men who had chased her that night. She turned around and looked into the pale cold eyes of Dane Bugden. So, he was one of them.

Sarah took a salad and sat at a table with two female students she'd become friendly with. When she finished her meal, she returned to the queue for coffee. Carrying it back, she was aware of Bugden's icy stare. As she levelled with his table a foot came out. She tripped, fell forward and dropped the cup. She quickly got to her feet, shaking from both shock and rage. She was about to slam her fist into the smirking jaw when a young man stepped in front of her, grabbed Bugden by the shirt collar and pulled him to his feet. 'I saw what you just did, clean up the mess and buy the lady another coffee.'

'Says who?' Bugden shook himself free of the grip, growled 'fuck off,' and strode out of the room.

'Are you okay?'

She looked into the intense brown eyes of her rescuer. He was copybook tall, dark and handsome.

'Thank you, yes.'

'Let me buy you a coffee.'

That was the beginning of her lovely relationship with Aaron Grant. From that time onwards, Bugden stayed away.

*

After they graduated, she and Aaron dated for two years. He was her first and only real love. They were about to announce their engagement when the phone call came. It was Aaron's mother, Sandra. Her voice was quiet and agitated. 'Sarah, something terrible has happened.' She strangled a sob. 'Aaron has had an aneurism.'

'Tell me he's going to be okay,' Sarah pleaded.

'You had better come to the hospital, he's in Prince Alfred.'

She was paralysed with fear as she made her way to the hospital. 'Please don't let him die,' she prayed.

Aaron was in intensive care and linked with tubes to a machine. Sandra was by his bed holding his hand, her face pale and soaked with tears. She looked at Sarah with distraught eyes but said nothing. Aaron's father Colin stood nearby. He nodded to Sarah, and left the room with a hand to his face. She went to the other side of the bed. 'What's happening?' was all she could whisper.

Sandra choked on her words. 'He's brain-dead. We have to turn off the machine.'

'No, you can't,' Sarah cried. Sandra shook her head slowly and kissed Aaron's cheek.

'You can't, Sandra.'

'He's gone love,' Sandra sobbed.

'But people survive aneurisms. He's only twenty-five.'

'This one was major. It wiped everything out.'

Sarah collapsed her head on Aaron's chest. 'Come back Aaron, come back,' she pleaded.

At Aaron's funeral, she met up with some of the people they had graduated with, all in uniform and forming a guard of honour as Aaron was carried from the church.

A dog barked in the distance and a passing motorist sounded his horn. It all seemed very normal, just like any other day, but for Sarah, that moment felt like the end of the world. The tears she held back during the service were welling in her eyes. To stop their downpour, she lifted her head and looked up at the sky. A blanket of clouds hung there. She tried to focus on them, anything to take her away from the present nightmare. As the blanket moved slowly, Sarah noted it was made up of hundreds of small shapes each resembling a splotch of clotted cream. She would never forget that weird sky 'till the day she died.

CHAPTER 11

Ellington punches in Pastor Allenby's phone number and is irritated to get the answering service preceded by the tunes of a familiar hymn, the name of which he can't remember. He then tries the Seymours' number and is further irritated by another answering machine. He looks at the names of the church people in Elise's address book. The only one showing a phone number is Maude Tingwell, the woman who was not at the church service because of her advanced debility.

'Mrs Tingwell?'

'Yes, who is that?' The voice is loud and croaky.

'Detective Ellington, I'm investigating the disappearance of Elise Seymour.'

'Who?'

'Elise Seymour.'

'Why haven't you found her?'

'We're working very hard. I'd like to talk to you about Elise. You might be able to help us.' Ellington shouts.

'What was that?'

'I want to talk to you about Elise Seymour.'

'I don't know where she is. Why would I?'

'Could I come around and have a quick word Mrs Tingwell?' Ellington has decided deaf people do not make good informants over the phone.

'You can come any time. I don't go anywhere these days.' The phone goes dead before Ellington has a chance to reply.

'Ellington.' The voice is booming and belongs to the chief. 'There's been an accident at Summer Hill railway. A bloke went under a train at eight-thirty this morning. His belongings identify him as Richard Ballantyne.'

'Accident?'

'Not sure at this stage, the body's still on the line. Forensic is there now.'

It takes Ellington forty minutes to get to Summer Hill through rush hour traffic going in both directions. The incident has thrown the rail transport system into chaos. Buses have been organised to convey commuters to their various destinations and the last of them rattles down the street with its full load of irate passengers. Two ambulances are parked directly outside the station. As Ellington descends the stairs, a stretcher manned by two ambulance officers conveying a shrouded shape passes him on its way up. He resists the temptation to lift the sheet and check the identity. Instead, he approaches the small group of uniformed police watching the two forensic people packing away their gear on the rail line. The mid-morning sun catches the blood glistening on the metal track. The train driver is on a bench jabbering incoherently to a female ambulance officer. Ellington addresses the most senior-looking member of the police group and shows his ID. 'DS Ellington, South Sydney. I'm investigating a missing person from this area. Richard Ballantyne is, was, a person of interest in the case. What happened here?'

'Sergeant Peter Hughes, Summer Hill police,' the man announces officiously. He fixes his eyes on the bloody railway track as he speaks. 'The man fell under the eight-thirty just as it pulled into the station. It appears there is only one witness.' Sergeant Hughes speaks in a sing-song voice, the same he'll undoubtedly use in the many media interviews he'll be giving over the next twenty-four hours.

'What did this witness see?'

'He saw the victim fall off the platform seconds before the train arrived.' Hughes jerks his head in the direction of a man standing a few metres away. 'That's him over there.'

The forensic pair is now on the platform walking towards the group. Ellington steps forward blocking their way. In spite of the baggy plastic forensic suit, he recognises Ivana Mirakoff. Ellington silently ponders the question: *what is a lovely young woman doing in such a horrendous job?*

'Good morning doctor. What can you tell me?'

The girl answers in a voice that could be detailing a weather forecast. 'Death instantaneous, massive trauma to the torso and upper legs, and an injury to the head, at this stage, it's impossible to say whether he fell, tripped or was pushed. We'll know more when we do the autopsy.'

'When will that be?'

'Later today.'

'Could you let me know the results?'

'Of course.'

Ellington rejoins the police and addresses Hughes. 'How was the deceased identified?'

'His briefcase is undamaged. The papers inside indicate the owner is Richard Ballantyne, an employee of Globe 50 Real Estate at Croydon.'

Ellington wanders over to the witness and introduces himself.

The man responds wearily. 'Joshua Trickett.'

'Could you tell me exactly what happened, and what

you saw Mr Trickett?'

'I've already told all that to the other police.' He nods in the direction of the three policemen who are still standing in the same spot.

'I know, but *I* need to hear it.'

Trickett sighs and speaks in a low voice. 'I took up my usual place on the platform, which is around there.' He points to an area a few metres away. 'I opened up my newspaper and started reading. The guy that died stood just over there.' Trickett waves an indicating hand. 'He always gets off at Croydon, same as me. That's why we both stand up this end of the platform. We often nod to each other, but have never talked.'

'So, you were reading your newspaper and what was he doing?'

'I think he was reading his too.'

'When the train approached, what happened?'

'I folded up my paper and moved forward to the yellow line. I have no idea where he was at that point.'

'Were there any other people nearby?'

'No, we were the only ones.' He raises his head in thought. 'Hang on, there was someone else, a person'... he pauses.

'Go on.'

'I didn't take much notice at the time, but there was someone standing back there.' Trickett points to the area behind them. It was a bit funny because he was wearing something, now I come to think, was a bit unusual.'

'Like what?'

'A sort of raincoat with a hood, weird, there wasn't a cloud in the sky.'

'Man or woman?'

'Don't know. When I saw him, he had his back to me.'

'You keep saying, *him*. So, you think it was a man?'

'No. It could have been a woman.'

'Do you know what the victim was doing?'

'No. I told you, I had no idea what he was doing at that exact moment. Anyway, I was just watching the train coming, and then just as it's here, out of the corner of my eye I see the bloke sort of stumble forward and fall off the platform right in front of the train. It was awful.'

'Did it look like he was pushed, jumped or just fell?'

'Like I said, he seemed to stumble. I don't know how else to put it.'

'Thanks, Mr Trickett. You'd better tell the Summer Hill police about the person in the raincoat if you haven't already.' Ellington takes down Trickett's details and turns to the train driver who is being helped to his feet by the ambulance officer. Ellington approaches and shows his ID.

'How is he?'

'He'll be coming with us. He's had a bad shock.' The woman is tall and athletic. Her dark hair is pulled back into a pony tail. Her plain features are somewhat relieved by a pair of expressive brown eyes.

'Can I ask him just a question or two?'

'Just a question or two and then we're off.' She pulls her charge back to the bench and they sit.

Ellington sits on the other side of the driver and introduces himself. The man nods and bows his head into his wide thick chest. His huge hands are linked together hugging his trembling knees.

'I know you've had a dreadful shock and I won't take too much of your time.' Ellington pauses and feels like a cad to be asking the poor bugger anything. It's clear he's in shock. 'Could you tell me just what you saw as you approached the area of the accident?'

'I told the other police. I saw nothing unusual until suddenly in the blink of an eye this bloke springs off the platform and goes under my train. I killed him.'

'You could do nothing to avoid what happened.' Ellington tries to force an encouraging smile. 'You said the man sprang out in front of you. What do you mean exactly?'

'Almost like he was flying.'

The ambulance officer interrupts. 'I think that's enough. Mr Melino needs medical assessment. We've wasted enough time.' She helps Melino to his feet and they shuffle off.

*

Ellington has just completed his report on the Ballantyne death when Chief Inspector Bellamy charges in. 'Forensic has just called. They need formal identification of this Ballantyne guy. The people at the Real Estate office have refused to do the deed.'

'Why?'

'Squeamish. The manager's out and there are only the two girls in the office.'

'I met Ballantyne a few days ago. I'll go. I'd like to see what the good doctor thinks now that she's had a decent look at the body.'

'Do you think this is connected with the Seymour girl?'

'Possibly,' Ellington half closes his eyes, his mind travelling back over the events. His voice is low, speaks almost to himself. 'The train driver said Ballantyne almost flew out in front of the train. That doesn't sound like someone accidentally tripping.'

'Think he might have topped himself?'

'Don't know. Anything come from the television interview or the newspapers about the Seymour girl?'

'Nothing yet.'

An hour later, Ellington enters the City Coroners Court.

The building with its mustard-yellow facade spreads across a wide area fronting busy Parramatta Road. Ellington knows his way around and passes several unmarked doors before reaching the office of Dr Ernest King, a senior pathologist. The man has aged badly in the six months since Ellington last saw him...tall, thin and stooped, he could be something out of a macabre spooky movie. His gaunt grey face seems to reflect the numerous dark, gruesome cavities he's peered into over the years.

'Glad to see you, Detective. All the identification we have is the briefcase found lying near the tracks.'

'I was half expecting to see Dr. Mirrakoff. She was attending at the scene.'

'Ah, the delightful Ivana. She assisted at the autopsy, but alas, has left. Sorry, you'll have to deal with this old codger.'

Ellington follows King through the mazes of corridors into the mortuary. King selects one of the steel boxes, pulls out the trolley, and flips back the top part of the sheet revealing the still handsome face of Richard Ballantyne, unscathed apart from a wound high on the forehead. King looks at Ellington, inquiringly.

'That's Richard Ballantyne,' says Ellington staring hard at the face.

King nods drops the sheet, and pushes the trolley back into its freezing home.

'The wound on the forehead........'

'Come back to my office and we can talk. It's not so cold,' King says.

The office is small and crowded with tall metal filing cabinets.

'Sorry I can't offer coffee or tea.'

'No worries. Just like to know what you think about the

head injury.'

'It occurred just prior to death, prior to the train passing over him. He must have hit his head on the track.'

'In your opinion, did Ballantyne fall, jumped or was pushed?'

'I don't think he jumped. I've had some experience with train suicides, and from witness reports, the victims have all jumped feet first. It's apparently a natural instinct, but of course, it's not out of the question for a person to go head first. It's just not usual.' King half closes his eyes and leans back in his chair. The deceased suffered massive injuries to the torso down to the legs.'

'The train driver said Ballantyne seemed to fly off the platform.'

'That, and the head wound suggest he went head first.'

'If his head was on the track how come it was intact?'

'The head hit the far rail. The impetus of the fall pushed the body forward thus moving the head and shoulders off the track.'

The late afternoon traffic is dense as Ellington drives back to the station. His mind is on Ballantyne. If he was murdered, who and why? He needs to see the railway station's CCTV footage. He'll do that tomorrow.

*

Summer Hill Police station is a converted house in a street on the far side of the railway line. Its blue/black bricks and glassed-in front veranda harmonise with the other Californian bungalows in the street. The entrance is in the side passage and the front reception desk is part of one huge room formed after many walls were demolished. Within minutes, Sergeant Hughes has set them up with the video from the railway station's CCTV footage. Ellington and Sarah sit side by side gazing intently at the screen. Hughes stands behind giving a commentary:

'The camera at the top of the stairs films the people passing through the gate about to make their descent. The clock in the background shows the time at twenty-one minutes past eight.'

They watch in silence as numerous people come and go through the footage.

'There's the witness, Joshua Trickett,' Hughes mutters. Trickett is carrying a briefcase and has a newspaper tucked under his arm. They watch as he passes out of view. Three minutes later Rick Ballantyne arrives.

'There's Ballantyne,' says Ellington. Ballantyne also carries a briefcase and newspaper. Two minutes later a hooded figure passes through the gate. Sarah gasps. Ellington hits the pause button. 'There's our caped mystery man. He knows about the camera. See how he has his head turned away.'

'Hard to tell if it's male or female.'

'Yes, the hood hides the face well and the cape hides the body.'

'I wouldn't call it a cape. It's more a cloak. Superman wears a cape,' Sarah suggests.

'Okay, a cloak.'

Hughes loads the second video which had filmed the area near the base of the stairs. The cloaked figure appears in the frame. 'See? He knows he's approaching another camera and his head is turned away,' Hughes observes.

'Is there a camera further up the platform, near where the incident happened?' asks Sarah.

'Apparently not, but I'll fast forward to when the suspect is returning to the stairs.' The tape runs for a few seconds before Hughes stops it. 'This should be around the time of the incident.' They watch as people pass the camera and then the hooded figure appears. As the head is turned sideways, there is still no chance of seeing the face. 'He's running towards the stairs.'

'Yes, he's in a hurry. There are people descending the stairs but he's the only one ascending. Let's have a look at the first tape again.' Hughes replaces the video with the first one. They now see the figure at the top of the stairs. As it passes the gate, the head is well averted. The station's big clock shows eight thirty-two.

'We'll need to show this to the shopkeepers in Station Street.' Ellington turns to Sergeant Hughes, 'unless that's already been done.'

'We thought he could have gone down Dixon Street. It's a lot quieter, less chance of being seen. We did a door knock on Dixon, and later talked to the shopkeepers in Station Street, nothing.'

'You'd think someone would have noticed a person in that get-up,' observes Sarah.

'He could have left a car at the start of Dixon and driven off before being seen,' suggests Hughes. 'Although come to think of it, at that time of day, that area is all *no parking*.'

'Have you got this to the press?' Ellington points at the screen.

'Yes, but I'm not happy with the image. It's very grainy.'

'I can draw it. All I need is a plain sheet of paper and a good pencil,' Sarah offers.

Ellington grins at Sarah. 'You never fail to surprise. Okay Constable, see what you come up with. I think the frame of the suspect at the top of the stairs is probably the best one to copy.' He finds the frame and hits the pause button. Sarah sets to work.

Hughes motions Ellington to the other side of the room. He frowns as he speaks. 'You know, I'm a bit at a loss as to why you guys are looking for that missing girl. She's local, and the call reporting her missing came through here. We were all set the next morning to get cracking when we get notice from South Sydney that they'd be taking over.'

'The father is a politician and apparently has contacts in high places. Inspector Bellamy was instructed by upstairs to find Elise Seymour.'

Hughes shrugs, 'and now why the interest in this Ballantyne guy?'

'Ballantyne was the ex-fiancé of the missing girl. That's why we're involved with his death. I'd appreciate you keeping us in the loop with this investigation.'

'We've interviewed Ballantyne's flat-mate and searched through the deceased's things.'

'And?

'The bloke was pretty shocked and adamant that Ballantyne wouldn't have topped himself. He was on a high, making arrangements to travel to Europe. There was nothing in his belongings to suggest anything wrong, and his bank balance was extremely healthy. On top of that, there was the Harley. That'd be worth a dollar or two.'

'You saw the Harley?'

'Sure did.'

'Anything else?'

'We interviewed the people at Globe 50. They all said the same. Ballantyne was in the pink. Not likely he would have committed suicide. We'll be interviewing his ex-girlfriend, Tara Gresham. Probably do that tomorrow.'

'We'll be interviewing her again too. She's part of our investigation into Elise Seymour's disappearance.'

It takes Sarah less than fifteen minutes to draw a good likeness of the cloaked figure.

'Very good,' Ellington nods appreciatively. 'Where did

you learn to draw like that?'

'I've always been interested in art, had lessons when I was a kid.'

'I'd like a few copies.'

'No problem.' Hughes waves towards the copying machine. 'I'll let the press know we've got a decent pic.' He picks up the phone.

Ellington makes several copies of the drawing. 'While we're in the neighbourhood we should talk to the chemist again,' he says thoughtfully.

Catherine greets them cautiously. 'What's happening? Have you found her?'

'No. I'm afraid not, but I'd like to ask you and Mr Brown a few more questions.'

'Mr Brown is out. He should be back in an hour.'

'He leaves you with it all?'

'I'm getting used to it. If anyone wants a prescription, they either come back later or it gets delivered to them.'

'Where is he?'

'I've no idea, but if you don't find Elise soon, I think Mrs Seymour will completely fold up.'

Ellington widens his eyes. 'You've spoken to her?'

'She came in a few days after Elise disappeared. She wanted to know what happened that last day, anything that Elise said or did that might throw some light.'

'And you told her what?'

'Exactly what I told you, how upset Elise was when talking with Rick and how quiet she was after that.' Catherine starts rearranging some items on the nearby table before speaking again. 'Mrs Seymour looked as if she was falling apart, she's utterly devastated. Now that a week's passed since Elise disappeared, I can only imagine how she must feel.'

Ellington unfolds Sarah's drawing. 'Are you aware that Rick Ballantyne was run over by a train yesterday, here in Summer Hill?'

'Of course, the accident was all around the street by nine o'clock. I mean we didn't know who had actually died until this morning.'

'Did you happen to see this person yesterday between eight and eight thirty-five?'

Catherine frowns as she studies the drawing. She shakes her head slowly. 'The local police were in here with the same question. Who is it?'

'We don't know, but we need to talk with him or her. You're sure you haven't seen this person, ever?'

'It's impossible to tell who it is under that outfit.'

Ellington draws in a deep breath. 'Catherine, can you tell me anything at all that might help us find Elise.'

Sarah interrupts. She speaks gently. 'The morning Elise talked to Rick, you said she was crying.'

'Yes, she was.'

'You said she came in and didn't talk.'

'Yes, she came in, put on her coat and changed her shoes....'

'She changed her shoes?' Ellington interrupts.

'Yes, she always wore her joggers here and carried her shoes in her bag. She said walking in high heels gave her blisters. She liked looking nice and wouldn't want the customers seeing her in her joggers.'

'You're certain she did this every day...wore her joggers?'

'Every day.'

'That's very interesting, we might come back later.'

Outside Sarah can't control her curiosity. 'What is it about the joggers?'

'Janet Seymour said Elise went off that morning in her high-heeled black court shoes. If she wasn't wearing her joggers, there must have been a reason.'

'Maybe you should just double-check with Mrs Seymour. She could have missed something.'

'I will.'

Sarah checks her watch. 'Feel like talking to the coffee shop people again?'

'Need a fix, constable?'

'You could say that.

*

'I'm betting the person in the cloak pushed Ballantyne.' Sarah sips her coffee. 'Why else would he go running up the stairs only seconds after someone had gone under a train?'

'I tend to agree.'

'What now?'

'I have to pay a visit to Maude Tingwell.'

'Who is?'

'The lady Elise tended Tuesdays and Fridays. We might as well do it now while we're in the area.'

Maude Tingwell's house is a semi-detached in a neglected part of Summer Hill. Waiting at the door gives Ellington and Sarah time to note the house's state of dilapidation. A whirring sound on the other side gives way to a loud crash. Finally, the door opens and a large elderly lady with a shock of white hair glares up at them from a wheelchair.

'What do you want?'

'Detective Sergeant Ellington and this is Constable Bradley. I phoned you yesterday.

'Come in, come in.' Maude Tingwell swivels her wheelchair around and steers it slowly along the narrow, sour smelling hallway. Ellington and Sarah follow. They arrive at a small, dimly lit sitting room. Maude swivels her chair to face them. 'This is about Elise?' she asks sternly.

'Yes,' Sarah says.

'Sit down, sit down.' Maude orders. 'What do you want from me?'

Ellington sits uncomfortably on a sinking leather lounge chair and Sarah perches on the edge of a small dining chair.

'Elise Seymour came to you Tuesday and Friday nights. Correct?'

'That's right.' The small watery eyes stare unwaveringly hard at Ellington.

'And she came Tuesday last week?'

'That's right.'

'How long had Elise been coming here twice weekly?'

Maude looks to the ceiling for inspiration. She wrinkles her brow and taps her nose. 'Six months? Perhaps nine months?'

'Can you be more specific?'

'No, I can't. I'm ninety-two years of age, and six months is much the same to me as nine months.'

Ellington smiles indulgently. 'Let's take a ballpark figure and say she was coming here for approximately seven months.'

Maude nods, 'approximately.'

'What time did she come?'

'Just after six.'

'And while she was here, what happened?'

'She made my dinner. Well, not exactly, she brought one of those frozen meals, popped it in the microwave and put it on a plate.'

'She didn't eat with you then?'

'She used to. She used to bring two frozen dinners and we would eat them together and then we'd watch telly and she'd stay 'til around nine. But all that stopped.'

'What happened?'

'She'd just serve me my dinner and leave.'

'What time would she leave?'

'A bit after six thirty.'

'So how long ago did this change take place?'

'Eight weeks, nine weeks, I don't know.'

'Did she say why she couldn't stay?'

'Something about helping another parishioner.'

'Was Elise in any way different the last time she came here?'

'Not at all.'

'Were you expecting her on Friday?'

'No. Someone phoned that morning saying Elise wouldn't be coming that night.'

'Who was this caller?'

'I don't know, they didn't give a name.'

'Man or woman?'

'Don't know. I don't hear well on the phone.'

'Thank you, Mrs Tingwell. Who is looking after you now that Elise isn't?'

'No one, are you volunteering?'

'I'm sorry. I can't personally, but if you like, I can refer you to one of the groups in the area who care for debilitated people.'

'Don't bother, I can manage. On the days Elise doesn't come, I get meals on wheels, and once a month someone comes and swishes a mop around.'

Ellington and Sarah see themselves out. 'She doesn't look well cared for. Did you see all that dust?' Sarah frowns.

'I intend calling those Home Care people. There's no way she can look after herself, and whoever's swishing a mop around, isn't doing a very good job.'

CHAPTER 12

Although it's very early summer, the days and nights are warm and humid. Ellington wakes hot and clammy. He throws off his sweaty sheet and springs out of bed. Amazing! He hasn't had a single nightmare since the Elise Seymour case began. He goes to the window and peers out. A warm breeze drifts in and the sky is a brilliant cloudless blue. Today is the day he will try out his new surfboard.

An hour later he's on Bondi Beach looking sadly at the flat ocean. His gleaming white and gold surfboard lies neglected on the sand. He's entertaining the idea of a body-surf, when his thoughts are interrupted by a familiar voice.

'Nice looking board.'

Ellington's eyes begin at the bright blue surfboard propped against a pair of well-shaped legs, then wander slowly upwards to a brief blue bikini and finally to honey coloured hair curling around a small smiling face.

'Sarah! What are you doing here?'

'It's a public beach, isn't it?'

'I didn't know you surfed.'

'Lots you don't know about me,' she laughs. 'The waves are shit.' She plonks down beside him. 'Been here long?'

161

'Crack of dawn.'

They sit silently looking out at the clear blue ocean sparkling under the melting sun.

'Going home soon?' he asks.

'Suppose so. Have you had breakfast?'

'No. I was in too much of a hurry getting here.'

'There's a place down the road, serves fish and chips to die for.'

'I didn't bring a change.'

'At this place, everyone eats in their swimmers. It's the rule.'

The busy cafe is just across from the beach. There are no enclosing walls, and the tangy smell of the sea envelopes them. The atmosphere is free and easy. Most of the patrons are either in their swimming costumes or in light beach clothing.

'Going to church tomorrow?' Sarah grins as she draws her soda through a straw.

'As a matter of fact, I am.'

'I was kidding.'

'I know you were, but I've got some unfinished business there. Pastor Allenby has some questions to answer, plus I have to check if he's observing my warning about social distancing.'

Their fish and chips arrive, and apart from Sarah's occasional '*yummy*', they eat in silence. While waiting for their coffee Sarah asks: 'What are you going to ask Allenby?'

'Why he's lying, and what happened at Dunkley.'

'Think you'll get the truth?' Sarah doesn't wait for Ellington's reply. 'Why don't you just call Dunkley yourself?'

*

'Dunkley Anglican Office, Carol speaking.' The voice is bright and chirpy.

'Good afternoon, Carol, Detective Sergeant Ellington from South Sydney Police. I'm wondering if I could speak with the Minister in charge, please.'

'That's Father Tovey.' I'm afraid he's not here at present. Can I help?'

'Perhaps you can. I'm inquiring about a Gregory Allenby who was pastor there a year or so ago.'

The woman's cheery tone flattens. 'What do you want to know about Allenby?'

'Why he left the church in Dunkley?'

'He didn't leave, he was kicked out.'

'You knew him personally?'

'I've been secretary here for twenty years. I know all about Dunkley and most of the people here.'

'Why was he kicked out?'

'He raped a young girl, that's why.'

'Can you give me the details? I know talking on the phone is difficult and I could drive out there.'

'That's probably not necessary. There's no one about just now, I'm able to talk.' There's a brief silence before Carol continues. 'Allenby was here for only a short time before there was trouble. He upset a lot of people. For starters, he drank too much, his sermons were a load of garbage and worst of all he had a liking for young girls. The last straw was when he raped young Kellie Bramston in the parsonage. There was a witness who saw Kellie running out of there in a terrible state, hysterical, her clothes torn. Allenby was charged. He denied everything, accused Kellie of lying and got himself a top lawyer. But it never came to trial. Kellie dropped the charge.'

'Why did she do that?'

'She thought it would be bad for the church, and she was uncomfortable about speaking in public about such a personal thing. But she only dropped the charge when the bishop promised her that Allenby would be defrocked and never allowed to carry on ever again as a minister.'

Ellington takes a deep breath. 'Thanks Carol, you've been very helpful.'

'Has he done it again?'

'Nothing's certain at this stage.'

Ellington drops the phone onto his coffee table and picks up Elise's photo album. He wanders onto his south facing patio and stretches out on the deck lounge. His eyes linger on the first photo as he studies the girl's face. The mouth is smiling but the eyes are sad. She's so beautiful. Although he hasn't had a single nightmare since this case began, he's still having vivid dreams. Looking at the photo, he's reminded of last night's dream.

He's in a fantasy world full of pink clouds and flying angels. He's dancing with Elise to the music of Nat King Cole's 'Somewhere along the Way.' He's holding her tightly as they move slowly through the clouds in time with the lovely music. He feels the soft pressure of her body against his and smells her rose scented hair.

The dream had ended abruptly when *'Somewhere along the Way'* took on the irritating beep of his alarm clock. He had unsuccessfully tried to capture more of the dream and wished it hadn't been interrupted. What's happening to him? Is he becoming obsessed?

*

Ellington decides to get to the church before the service finishes and catch Allenby if he'd ignored last week's warning. He is surprised to find the service finished, and only a few people in the house. Most are in the yard with their tea and scones. He sees Seymour chatting with two elderly ladies. His mind goes into overdrive as he tries to recollect their names.

'Ah, detective, have we found a convert here?' Esther Raymond's voice ripples across as she winds her way slowly toward him.

'Morning Mrs Raymond, no I'm not ready for salvation just yet. I need to talk with you all again though, check to see if anyone has heard from Elise'.

Esther shakes her head sorrowfully. 'We are still praying and hoping. Have you unearthed anything at all?'

'Afraid not.'

'Well, her disappearance has affected everyone quite badly. Poor Pastor Allenby is so upset. He couldn't deliver his sermon this morning. It was such a shame to see. His homilies are always so inspirational. He just stood there, blinking. I think he was trying not to cry.'

'I must have a word with him. Excuse me.'

Allenby has moved to the back terrace. Ellington's shoes sink into the damp grass as he walks across.

'Mr Allenby, could I have a word?'

Allenby's contrived smile gives way to a pained, grim expression as Ellington approaches him.

'Is there somewhere quiet?'

'You could come to my sitting room.'

The small room has an open window which allows a soft breeze. It's an austere room, with only a desk, some chairs and a loaded bookcase. The furnishings are iill-matched and there's a faint smell of cigarette smoke hanging in the air. Allenby sits behind his desk and gravely surveys Ellington. 'I did what you suggested last week... some people stayed in the house and the rest in the yard. I conducted the service at the veranda door.'

'Pleased to hear it.' Ellington sits opposite Allenby. 'That's not what I wanted to talk about. Elise's diary tells us that she was coming here every Tuesday and Friday for the past nine or so weeks. Is that right?'

Allenby's eyes narrow and he hesitates before speaking. 'Yes.'

'Why did you lie to me?'

Allenby draws in a deep breath, exhales and looks past Ellington, not willing to meet his eyes. 'I didn't lie.'

'You failed to tell me then.'

'I didn't deny Elise was helping with my sermons.'

'You said she'd only done this on a few occasions.'

Allenby swallows, his prominent Adam's apple jerks up and down. He closes his eyes for several seconds, opens them slowly and speaks harshly. 'When I left Dunkley and came to this parish, I learned very quickly that my congregation was ultra-conservative. They formed the church specifically to hear what they wanted to hear.'

'You failed to tell the people here what had happened in Dunkley'.

'I thought they knew.'

'They didn't.'

Allenby's eyes examine the ceiling before fixing on Ellington. 'After the incident in Dunkley, I seemed to have lost my flair. I had trouble writing the sermons they wanted to hear. Elise has a gift. She writes with inspiration.'

'Why did she lie to everyone about where she was?'

'Lie?'

'She told her parents she was at Maude Tingwell's'.

'She *was* at Maude's.'

'Not for long. Most of the time she was here, with you.'

'I asked her not to tell anyone. I thought it wouldn't look good. When I was in Dunkley, there were lies spread around about me. A girl there caused me a great deal of trouble. I lost my ministry. I was shunned. I didn't want that to happen again.'

166

'You were accused of rape.'

'I denied it vigorously. It was the girl's word against mine... until she found a witness who lied for her.'

'And?'

'This so-called witness said he saw the girl running from the parsonage. Her clothes were torn and she was crying.'

'You denied it?'

'Of course, I was at home that night, alone. No one came to my house, I swear it.' Allenby rises from his seat and walks to the window, looking out. 'I think someone else raped her, and for some unknown reason she blamed me.'

'Why would she do that?'

'I had previously reprimanded her for her loose behaviour, and I suspect she might have been getting back at me, and protecting her attacker at the same time. I believe he was probably the misfit she'd been seeing.'

'Why protect him?'

'Maybe she was still infatuated with him. Anyway, someone did rape her. She ended up in the local hospital and the examination apparently showed rape. They contacted the police. That's when I was arrested. At the eleventh hour the girl dropped the charges, but Sergeant, as you know, dirt sticks. That's why I asked Elise not to mention to anyone that she was coming to my house. As soon as that was made public, there'd be a storm coming from Dunkley. There are spies in every town, especially Sydney.

'If you needed Elise to write your sermons, couldn't she just do that at her home and send them to you?'

'She often did prepare them before coming. We would discuss them together and sometimes I'd make little changes. Her coming here meant a lot to me.'

'But why two nights?'

'She liked coming. I made her a nice dinner. She was glad to have a break away from her parents.'

'That's not what she wrote in her diary.'

Allenby juts his chin, and glares at Ellington. 'What *did* she write?'

'She wrote that you had been pestering her and that she was thinking of stopping her visits.' Ellington lets his words sink before continuing. 'She also said someone had raped her.' Allenby's eyes widen and his jaw clenches.

'God no, who?'

'She didn't say, but I must ask you, where were you on the night of Tuesday thirteenth of November?'

Allenby's bloodshot eyes dart around the room before settling uneasily on Ellington. 'I'll have to check my diary.' He opens a book on his desk and turns the pages. 'That was the Tuesday before last. I was expecting Elise, she always comes on Tuesdays. She didn't turn up.'

'Did she phone, cancelling?'

'No. I'd organised dinner, I was quite let down. It was the first time that had ever happened.'

'Did you try contacting her to find out why she didn't turn up?'

'I tried phoning her mobile, but it was turned off.'

'You didn't call her parents?'

'That would have been awkward.'

'Do you have any witnesses to support your whereabouts that night?'

'I stayed at home, and had my dinner alone. I watched television and went to bed around ten. You can't think I would do such a thing.'

Ellington walks to the doorway, hovers there a few seconds, and then says: 'Did you know Elise's ex-fiancé, Richard Ballantyne, was run over by a train last Thursday?'

'I heard it. You don't think there's any connection?'

'It's very possible. Did Elise ever discuss Ballantyne with you?'

'I think she might have.'

'And what *might* she have said?'

'She said he broke her heart.'

'And how did you react to that?'

'I felt great sorrow for her.'

'Did she ever mention Tara Gresham?'

'Yes. She told me how the girl had deceived her. Poor Elise is so vulnerable. Those so-called friends were despicable.'

'It's likely I will need to speak with you again. Please don't leave Sydney without advising me.'

Ellington walks out into the sunlight and approaches Janet Seymour.

'Good morning.'

'Is it? There's nothing good in this world without my daughter.'

'You know about Richard Ballantyne?'

'Yes.'

'We think there could be a connection between his death and Elise's disappearance.'

'How?'

'I'd like to come around and have another look in Elise's room.'

'Very well, if you must.'

'After church?'

Janet Seymour nods sullenly.

Once again Ellington is transported to a magical place lost in the depths of time, a place of peace and calm, a place that belongs to the distant past. The little glass angels tinkle above the bed as the warm breeze stirs them and ruffles the sweet-smelling potpourri hanging from the bed posts. Ellington disengages himself from the spell that's engulfing him and opens the wardrobe. He notes the shoes lined up on the floor of the robe. There are two pairs of sandals, a pair of slippers, a pair of joggers and at least fifteen pairs of dress shoes in every imaginable colour.

*

Janet Seymour sits near the rose garden staring into space.

'Mrs Seymour, may I have a word?"

The woman gazes at him with sorrowful eyes and nods.

'How many pairs of joggers does Elise have?'

'Just the one pair.'

'When you waved Elise off to work that morning, you said she was wearing her red dress and black court shoes.'

'That's right.'

'The girl at the chemist shop said Elise always wore her joggers to work and then changed into her good shoes. Didn't you think it unusual that Elise wasn't wearing her joggers that morning?'

A deep frown creases Janet Seymour's forehead. She speaks slowly. 'It didn't mean anything to me at the time.'

'Did you have any idea that Elise visited Gregory Allenby every Tuesday and Friday?'

Janet's head jerks upward, her body tense. 'No,' she whispers.

'She was helping him with his sermons apparently.'

Janet remains silent, and looks into her hands.

'In her diary, she wrote that someone raped her, the Tuesday before she disappeared. Did she confide in you or your husband?'

Janet plunges her head into her hands. 'God, no, she

170

Missing In Red

never said a word.'

CHAPTER 13

'At last, we've had a response to the papers... from Sea Haven of all places. A bloke in a cafe up there saw someone matching Elise Seymour's photo. Saw her on Thursday the fifteenth, with a man.' Chief Inspector Bellamy's face relaxes into a rare smile as he delivers the information to Ellington.

'Sea Haven? Where the hell's that?' Ellington asks.

'A small seaside village on the mid-coast.'

*

The Northern Freeway is a four-car carriageway that allows fast travel in heavy traffic. After two hours, a smoky vapour settles over the bushland on both sides. Gradually the dark pall in the sky increases and the smell of smoke fills the cabin. A road block sends them on a detour. Ellington groans. 'This'll add at least thirty minutes to the trip.'

It's nearly two before they reach their destination. Coming into the village of Sea Haven, they pass a sprinkling of timber cottages in various states of disrepair. Closer to town, the houses are prestigious, modern two-storey affairs with lots of glass and lush tropical gardens. The town proper comprises a single line of shops covering two blocks and set opposite a glittering lake. A large cafe takes prominent pride of place in the first block, its bright yellow facade winding around the corner.

'We're meeting our witness in there.' Ellington points at the cafe as they drive past.

The café is light and airy. Most of the customers are on the front balcony taking advantage of the beautiful weather. Ellington and Sarah approach a heavily built, dark haired man stacking glasses behind the counter.

Ellington announces: 'Detective Sergeant Ellington and Senior Constable Bradley.' They show their IDs. 'We'd like to talk to Joe Mousseff.'

'That's me.'

Ellington places the photo of Elise on the countertop.

'Was this the girl you saw here?'

'Sure looks like her.'

'And she was with a man?'

'Yeah, a guy with ginger hair.'

'When exactly did you see them?'

'Thursday before last.'

'What time did they get here and leave?'

'I reckon it was about two when they came, and they stayed about half an hour.'

'Anyone else recognise her?'

'Dunno, you could ask Janie.' He jerks his head in the direction of a tall skinny girl lazily swishing a Wettex over a laminated table.

'She would've been on that day.'

'Did you hear any of their conversation?'

'Nah, the guy came to the counter and ordered the coffees. I wasn't anywhere near their table, wouldn't know what they were talking about. Janie might have heard something'.

'You had never seen either of those people before?'

'Right on. Reckon I know just about everyone in this

'ere village. Never saw either of them before.'

'Thanks. We'll talk with Janie, okay?'

'Sure.'

The girl wears a vacant expression along with a tiny tight black skirt, a skimpy white top and an arrangement of colourful tattoos.

Ellington unfolds the photo of Elise. 'Your boss remembers seeing this girl or someone who looks like her. Do you remember seeing her?'

Janie studies the photo with screwed up eyes. 'I kinda remember seeing a girl that looked a bit like that.'

'Your boss thought it was Thursday before last.'

She scratches her head with her free hand and absently rubs the Wettex across the table with the other. 'Jeez, how'd you expect me to remember that far back?'

Sarah breaks in. 'You said you saw a girl who looked a bit like the one in this photo. What exactly do you mean when you say the girl looked a *bit* like this one?'

'Well, it's hard to tell. She wasn't dressed like that for a start.'

'How *was* she dressed?'

'Just normal, I mean, look at that dress, wow!'

'Let's forget about the dress, could the girl you saw, be the girl in this photo?' Ellington stabs at the photo.

'Not real sure,' she stares again at the photo and bites her bottom lip.

'Why not?' groans Sarah.

''Cause that week I'd lost one of me contacts and wasn't seeing proper.'

'What about the man she was with, do you know him?'

'Sorry, I don't remember the guy, but I do know one thing.'

Ellington and Sarah wait with raised eyebrows.

'I'd never seen either of them before.'

'How do you know that, if you didn't have your contacts in?' Sarah is losing patience.

'Look, I know when locals come in, they all say g'day. This pair said nothin'. That's how I know.'

'Thanks, Janie. If either of those two people come here again, please contact me.' Ellington hands the girl his card.

'While we're here Sarge, we might as well have some lunch.'

'Good idea.' They stroll back to the counter. 'If you see either of those people again, please contact me.' Ellington hands Joe his card. 'And I'll have a flat white and a ham and cheese melt. Constable Bradley will have.......?'

'I'll have the same.'

They eat their lunch on the balcony and gaze out at the lake. Sarah squeals with delight when she sees two big pelicans land with their surf-ski feet. 'I just love those big birds.'

'I'll give you one for Christmas, Constable.'

Sarah's face clouds, 'Could you not call me Constable, or Bradley, please?'

Ellington shifts from his comfort zone. 'What then?'

'Just Sarah.'

Ellington nods. 'Okay, from now on I will call you *Just Sarah.*'

Sarah appreciates Ellington's attempt at humour, but doesn't respond. After a few minutes, she says: 'What do you think of our witnesses?'

'Hard to say, Joe seemed pretty sure, but then maybe he's got something wrong with his sight too. Janie? Well, I don't think she knows what day of the week it is.' He glances at his watch. 'Before we drive back, I think we should talk to some of the shopkeepers.'

Missing In Red

They question the barber, the newsagent, the baker, the fruit shop and the butcher. None can recall seeing Elise. The hairdresser shop is the last on the line. A middle-aged woman with blond hair striped pink and green is shampooing an elderly customer. Ellington shows his ID and then the photograph of Elise. 'At any time in the past ten days did you happen to see this girl?' The woman's mouth works overtime on her wad of gum as she squints at the photo. 'Yeah, I think I saw her walking past the shop one day. I'd stepped outside for a fag and there they were, walking by.'

'They?'

'Yeah, she was with a guy.'

'When exactly was this?'

She purses her lips in thought. 'It was the week before last. The only reason I remember them was the girl reminded me of Marilyn Monroe.'

'And the man?'

'Didn't take much notice of him.'

Could you pinpoint the day?'

'It would have been Thursday or Friday.' She taps her forehead. 'Yeah, Mel works Thursdays and Fridays, and Mel was definitely here. I remember calling to Mel and telling her I'd just seen a Marilyn lookalike,' the woman grins.

'Did you see where they went?'

'Yeah, they boarded a car, parked just back from the corner.'

'Could you describe the car?'

'Red. Not real big, sedan.'

'Number plates?'

'Give us a break mate, my memory ain't that good.'

'Thanks, if you see either of them again, call me.' He hands her his card.

Outside, Ellington looks at his watch. He decides they

might make it back to Sydney before dark.

He misses the U-turn and travels on a kilometre looking for a way to turn back. A sign ahead announces the name of the next village. Ellington whistles, 'looks like we're coming into Lauraville.'

'So what?'

'Lauraville is the name of the town Travis Lockhart visited the day Elise disappeared. And Travis Lockhart has red hair.'

'That's a bit of a coincidence.'

'It certainly is.' Ellington drives into the town and parks in the quiet main street outside the news agency.

'This is as good a place as any to start.' They wander into the tiny shop. Packed shelving runs along both side walls, creating a crowded, confusing jumble. They manage to find the small counter and its only occupant, a thin elderly man reading a newspaper. He doesn't appear to be aware of their presence and when Ellington speaks, there's no response. Ellington and Sarah exchange quizzical glances. Ellington speaks again, louder. 'Good afternoon. Detective Sergeant Ellington.' He shows his ID. 'Could we have a word?'

The man raises bushy white eyebrows, looks at Sarah with rheumy eyes and smiles. 'Well, hello, didn't see you there. Police did you say?'

'Yes sir, we're investigating the disappearance of a young woman.'

'Heavens, I didn't know anyone was missing.'

'Not from here, Sydney.'

'Do you think she's up here?'

'It's possible, but we need to talk to the Lockhart family. Do you know them?'

'Jenny and Martin? Yes of course.'

'Can you tell me where they live?'

'I can indeed, but it won't do you any good.'

'Why is that?'

'They've gone away, overseas, I believe.'

'When did they go away?'

'Oh, more than a month ago.'

'Wasn't Mrs Lockhart ill?'

'Jenny? Not that I know of. She's a very fit lady, one of our top golfers. I saw her the day before they flew out. She looked the picture of health. She was so excited. It was their first big overseas holiday.'

Ellington raises his eyebrows, 'Anyone living in their house?'

'No. It's empty.'

'Do you know their son, Travis?'

'Travis left Lauraville years ago, boarding school in Sydney. Then he stayed there to do his university course. He was just a little kid when I last saw him.'

'We understand that Travis came to the house last week.'

'Did he?'

'Could you give me the address?'

The man scratches his head. 'They're around in Loftus Street. Hang on I'll look it up in the book.' He thumbs through the nearby phone book. 'Ah, here it is, thirty-one, Loftus. If you take the first street on your left, then the next on your right, that's Loftus.'

'Thank you, sir.'

The weatherboard house is set on a wide block with a front deck spanning the entire width of the house. The grass is overgrown, and straggly weeds compete with woody shrubs in the neglected garden. Ellington knocks on the front door. When there's no response they walk around to the back door, again no response. Ellington peers through the garage window. A white sedan sits next to a golf cart and a trailer.

'It might be worth talking to the neighbours.' The words are no sooner out of Ellington's mouth, when an elderly woman leans over the fence.

'The Lockharts are away. What do you want?'

'Police. We want to talk with Travis Lockhart. Have you seen him lately?'

'Travis was here week before last. He came on Thursday and left on Sunday. What's he done?'

'He may have information about a missing person. Did you speak to him while he was here?'

'I saw him arrive. I was over there collecting their post. I've been looking after their mail while they're overseas.'

'Did you speak to each other?'

'At first I didn't recognise him. It'd been a while since he's been up here. I said: *Who are you and what are you doing here?* He then told me who he was, and said he was having a short break from Sydney.'

'Did he have anyone with him?

'I didn't see anyone.'

'What time would that have been?

She frowns in thought. 'It would have been around two thirty. I'd just finished watching the midday movie.'

'You don't happen to have keys to the house, do you?'

'As a matter of fact, I do.' She looks at Sarah's uniform with a hint of hesitation.

'I'm Detective Sergeant Ellington, South Sydney Police and this is senior Constable Bradley.'

The woman nods. 'Well as you're the police, I don't suppose I can say no. Hang on, I'll get the key.'

The house is empty and all the rooms are clean and tidy. There's nothing to indicate current occupation.

'It looks like Travis was lying about at least one thing,

there's nothing wrong with his mother.'

Night is falling when Ellington drops Sarah back at the Station.

'See you tomorrow, *Just Sarah*.'

Sarah pulls a face and waves him off.

CHAPTER 14

December 2021

Ellington's mobile goes off just as he enters his apartment.

'Detective Ellington?' The female voice is shaky, fragile.

'Yes. Who is this?'

'It's Tara Gresham. I've just found a note in my letterbox and I'm scared.'

'Tell me, Tara.'

'It's written in red ink and it says: *You are next bitch. Hell is waiting for you.*'

'Are you at home?'

'Yes'.

'Alone?'

'Yes.'

'Is there a friend or family member you can get to come over?'

'No, all my family is in Victoria. There's really nobody I feel I can impose on.'

'Make sure all your doors and windows are locked. If anyone comes to the door, don't open it, unless it's someone you're absolutely sure about. You'll be at the office tomorrow?'

'If I'm still alive.'

'I'll see you around ten. Bring the note.'

*

Ellington is pleased to see Sarah already there when he arrives early at the station the next morning.

'Who would be threatening Tara Gresham?' she asks.

'Don't know. It seems all my suspects are getting themselves either murdered or threatened.'

'You suspect Tara?'

'She has a motive to kill Elise *and* Ballantyne.'

'So, you think Elise has been murdered?'

'There's no way of knowing, but it has to be considered.'

'If you think Elise is still alive, then surely, she has to be a suspect?'

Ellington shrugs. 'I'm going into the city to see Tara Gresham. Want to come?'

*

Tara leads them into the same conference room as before.

'Here's the note.' She hands Ellington a small slip of paper.

'You found this in your letterbox last night when you got home from work?'

'Yes. I called you straight away.'

'No ideas?'

'None.'

'I'll have it tested for prints. Yours and mine will be there, but it'll be interesting to see what else we find. Could you call into either Central Police or South Sydney and have your prints taken sometime today?'

'Guess I've got no choice.'

'Would you like some police protection?'

'You mean someone live with me?'

'That, or regular patrols around your area.'

182

'My unit's only a bed-sitter. I couldn't handle living there with a stranger, but I'd appreciate the regular patrols.'

'No worries, the patrols will start today.'

Ellington organises an examination of the note, sips a cup of instant coffee, and waits. The results come through quickly. The only prints on the note are those of his and Tara Gresham's. He takes his coffee to Sarah's desk and shares the information with her.

'You kind of expected that though, didn't you? Anything about the ink or stationery that might give a lead?' she asks.

'Just the sort of note paper and envelope you get in every supermarket in the country.'

'Do you think Tara might have written the note herself?'

'That has occurred to me. It's possible she killed Ballantyne in a fit of revenge. She thought Ballantyne had gone back to Elise. She could have thought Elise had staged her disappearance and was actually living with Ballantyne. You know the old saying...a woman scorned.'

'What about Travis Lockhart?' asks Sarah.

'Travis Lockhart is also now a person of interest. He too has a motive for killing Ballantyne and threatening Tara. He admits to visiting Lauraville but lies about his mother's illness. And the barista at Sea Haven said the girl in question was with a red-headed guy.' Ellington frowns. 'It'd be handy if we had a photo of him.'

'There's one in Elise's album.'

'You're kidding.'

'The last page, it's a photo of him and Ballantyne.'

'Well done, Sarah. I'll fax it up to Joe, and see if it fits.'

'Anything been done about patrolling Tara's neighbourhood?'

'Yes, all organised. They start this afternoon.'

*

183

Missing In Red

There's still light when Tara Gresham drives into her garage. On her way to the front door, she glances at the letterbox, hesitates a moment, and then flips open the lid. There are two letters, one's from a charity organisation. The other sends adrenalin shooting through her body. She hurries through the front door, turns on the light and tears at the envelope. There's the same bold red writing, but different words. *Time is running out for you. Hell is getting impatient.* She looks out the window and sees a police car cruising slowly past. Breathing a sigh of relief, she pulls the security chain across the door.

Ellington has downed his second scotch when his mobile goes off.

'It's Tara Gresham. There's been another one, came today. I'm frightened.'

'Patrols will be going past all night. Stay inside, keep your doors locked, and don't open up to anyone. Hear?'

'Yes. I heard.'

'You've got the patrol car's phone number?'

'Yeah, they dropped it in.'

'Good. I'll call you tomorrow.'

*

It's eight thirty when Ellington arrives at the station, and already the temperature has reached thirty degrees. Bush fires up and down the coast, are causing turmoil and distress, and the city is shrouded in smoke. Sarah is already at her desk, her coat hung over the back of the chair, her eyes fixed intently on the computer screen.

'Tara got another note yesterday.'

Sarah's eyebrows shoot up and her eyes widen as she swivels her chair to face him.

'Same person?'

'Looks like it.' Ellington leans over Sarah's shoulder

and peers at her computer screen. 'What are you up to?'

'Getting more information on Travis, his parents have lived in Lauraville for several years. He started at Sydney University three years ago. Law. He dropped out around the same time as Elise. Another coincidence?'

'The barista at Sea Haven said the guy with the Elise look-alike definitely could have been Lockhart.'

'Where do we go from here?'

'Elise wrote she was raped but didn't say who.'

'She thought someone was reading her diary.'

'Yes, and the bit about the rape was in code.'

'Do you think she imagined it? After all, she was bipolar she might have been having delusions.'

'Don't know. But it's time we talk again with both chemist Brown and Travis Lockhart.'

Catherine is attending to a customer when Ellington and Sarah enter the shop. They exchange glances, Catherine is hardly recognisable. No longer is she flouting the 'Marilyn Monroe' hairdo. All the curls have been replaced by straight lanky hair hanging around her collar. Gone are the brightly painted mouth and the fluttering mascara laden lashes. She looks pale and plain.

'Mr Brown in?' asks Sarah.

'In the dispensary,' Catherine says sullenly.

Nathan Brown is measuring pills into a small jar. He looks up, surprised. 'Have you found her?'

'No. But we'd like to go over a few things with you. Elise Seymour wrote a diary and there's an entry on the ninth of November that suggests you had more than just an employer's interest in her.'

'What nonsense.'

'I'd like you to tell us your whereabouts and movements on Tuesday evening the thirteenth of November.'

'Why? You don't think I had anything to do with Elise's disappearance, surely?'

'We can't ignore Elise's diary entry. An entry on Tuesday the thirteenth, just four days after, states that she had been raped.'

Brown swallows hard and shakes his head sadly. 'Raped? Elise had bipolar. Sufferers frequently have misunderstandings and incorrect interpretations of events. If she wrote that I had been making inappropriate advances, it was all in her mind.'

'I would still need to know where you were that night.'

'I was in my home, alone.'

'Can anyone support this?'

'I'm afraid not. I rarely go out and I rarely have guests. When she came to work on Wednesday, she said nothing to me about being raped. Maybe she talked about it with Catherine, you could ask her.'

'I will. Thanks.'

The customer has gone and Catherine is wrapping a package. Sarah whispers, 'Somehow, I don't think Brown is the rapist, he seems pretty upfront. Maybe Elise *did* imagine it.'

'I don't entirely agree. I think he knows something he's not telling. Let's talk to Catherine.'

Catherine's plump face contorts into a grimace when Ellington tells her about the rape. 'No, she definitely didn't say anything to me. Maybe that's what caused her sad mood on Wednesday. I thought it was Rick at the time.'

'Thanks, Catherine. If you think of anything, you've still got my card?'

*

Ellington finds Travis Lockhart dealing with a customer. He waits patiently for the conversation to finish and then draws him aside. 'I've been to Lauraville and spoken with a reliable witness. I was told that your parents are overseas and there's nothing wrong with your mother. It's fair to say you haven't been completely honest with me. I'd like the truth. What were your movements on the morning of Thursday the fifteenth November?'

Lockhart's eyes dart around the library and remain fixed on the shelving behind Ellington. 'I didn't lie about Lauraville. I did go there that Thursday and I stayed until late Sunday. Okay, I lied about my mother being ill. It was the only way I could get leave from the library at short notice. I was feeling stressed out and needed a decent break. My folks were away and I thought four days alone in a quiet place would get me back online.'

'You were seen in the Sea Haven coffee bar on Thursday the fifteenth with a young woman who, according to the barista, closely resembles Elise Seymour.'

'I had coffee there, but it wasn't with Elise.'

'Who was it then?'

'Look, now you mention it, the girl did look a bit like Elise. That is, before Elise had her hair cut and dyed black. But it wasn't Elise.'

Ellington takes out his notebook, poises his pen and stares hard at Lockhart.

'Her name please?'

'Ava.'

'Ava who?'

'I don't know her last name.'

'Where does she live?'

'I don't know, I only just met her. She was hitching, I gave her a lift. She was on her way up to Coffs. I bought her a coffee at the Sea Haven Cafe.'

'She was seen getting back into your car.'

'Yeah, I drove her back to the highway.'

'Did she give any indication as to who she was meeting at Coffs, or an address she'd be staying at?'

'No.'

'What did you talk about then?'

'We just talked about our backpacking holidays. I told her about mine up the Top End and she told me about hers in Tassie.'

'Nothing else?'

'That was it.'

'Mr Lockhart, unless you can supply me with this girl's identification, you will remain a person of interest in the disappearance of Elise Seymour.' Ellington puts away his notebook. 'Don't leave Sydney without advising us.'

CHAPTER 15

The morning brings more hot weather and reports of bushfires all over the country. Ellington dashes from his car and almost collides with Sergeant Geoff Murray at the Station's front doorway.

'G'day Duke, I'm on my way out to Bankstown, the Gallego case. We've got a reliable eye-witness, looks like we'll be making an arrest real soon.'

'What happened to that other eye-witness we had lined up?'

'Turned out a fizz.'

Ellington consults his watch and glances through the glass doors into the front office. He sees Bellamy strutting about but can't see Sarah. He makes a decision.

'Got room in your car for an interested onlooker?'

Murray grins. 'Plenty...the other guys have already left.'

As they drive, Ellington chews over what he'd planned for the day. Nathan Brown had become a thorn in his side and he'd decided to put him under surveillance. Now he must make an adjustment to his plans. He takes out his mobile. 'Sarah, 'I'm going with Geoff Murray to talk to an eye witness in the Gallego murder. I'd like you to do something for me.'

Sarah knocks on Chief Inspector Bellamy's door. 'Enter,' calls the deep gravelly voice.

'Detective Ellington has asked me to meet him at Summer Hill later today, the Seymour case. I need an unmarked car.'

Bellamy is sorting through papers, preoccupied. He speaks without looking up. 'Get Farrugia to help you with the car.'

'Thanks.'

Sarah finds Anthony Farrugia at his desk, and together they go to the downstairs car park. Farrugia is a tall gangly young man with straight black hair, a pair of huge hooded brown eyes and full lips set into a long narrow face. He wears a permanently startled expression and seems totally out of place in a police uniform. Sarah can better see him wearing a long white apron serving food or in a chef's hat cooking it.

'The Electra is available.' He points to a shiny, pale blue car wedged between two older vehicles. 'I'll get the keys.' He disappears into the small office at the back of the basement and returns with a set of keys. 'There's a kit in the boot, blue light, binoculars, rope, torch, cuffs all that stuff. All the cars are fitted with navigators.'

'Thanks.'

'No problem, just sign here.' He opens a log book, plants it on the bonnet, and points with a long thin finger. Sarah signs unlocks the door and slides into the driver's seat.

She has no difficulty finding her way to Summer Hill and is glad to see a parking spot directly opposite the chemist's shop. She removes her hat and puts on an oversized pair of sunglasses. She sees Catherine walking around the shop, but there's no sign of Brown. *Probably out in his dispensary,* she thinks. After ninety minutes she decides maybe she should make sure Brown *is* in the dispensary. She remembers the lane running behind the shops, and hopes it might provide some view into the pharmacy. She walks down the street and turns into the lane which runs between the back of the shops and the tall car-park fence. The putrid stink of rotting garbage and stale urine are overpowering. A window sits high on the plain brick wall of the pharmacy. Sarah drags a milk crate from behind next door's cake shop and climbs. It's just high enough for her to see into the dispensary. And there's Nathan Brown in the process of pasting labels on small plastic containers. He's intent on his task and doesn't look in Sarah's direction. As she thought, there's no door leading from the dispensary to the laneway, which means the only way for Brown to exit the shop is through the front entrance. She returns to her car and resumes her watch. At midday, she buys a sandwich from the deli and a coffee from the cafe.

At one, she's rewarded. Brown emerges and hurries down busy Station Street. Sarah watches until he's at the car park entrance. She then puts her car into action and waits near the entrance. She watches Brown hop into a car, and thinks: *Why am I not surprised the car is brown?*

She follows Brown at a safe distance and follows him through suburban back streets for eight minutes until they reach the nearby suburb of Canterbury. Brown turns into a driveway that runs uphill to a garage at the back. Sarah parks a few houses further down the street and walks back to the house. She sees Brown emerge from the garage, and walk to the back of the house. An hour later, Brown's car swings down the drive. Sarah looks at her watch. It's two o'clock. Why hasn't Ellington been in contact?

She walks up the steep driveway and checks the rear door and windows. All appear locked, apart from a small hopper-type window on the far side. Sarah slips her fingers under its base and pulls it towards her. She manages to get her hand onto the winder. She finds a small plastic stool propped against the garage wall, and using it to get through the window, slides into a small laundry.

Checking the cupboards, she finds the usual stuff…washing powder, insecticides, bleach and shoe polish. She wanders out into the hallway and into the kitchen. Sarah wrinkles her nose at the strong, unpleasant smell of stale cooking odours. A fat black cockroach scuttles over the pile of unwashed dishes which decorate the sink. A table with a red laminated top is covered with newspapers and more unwashed crockery. The linoleum on the floor is cracked and dirty. There is a small pantry containing an assortment of tinned food. Sarah checks through the cupboards and finds saucepans and frying pans in one, a stack of mismatched crockery in another, and cooking gadgets, plastic lunch boxes and piles of paper plates in the rest. The top three drawers are full of cutlery including a set of carving knives. The bottom drawer is stuffed with papers. Sarah sifts through them and finds most are bills and receipts. She moves onto the next room which turns out to be a large bedroom containing a queen bed, a bedside table and two old fashioned wardrobes. She finds nothing out of the ordinary apart from an opened packet of condoms in the bedside table. The first wardrobe is stacked with shirts, shorts and slacks. The second contains a row of suits, mostly brown, and a collection of shoes. A tennis racket with a broken string stands forlornly in one corner and an empty suitcase stands in another. The bathroom is even dirtier than the kitchen. The vanity cupboard contains medications, mainly analgesics and sleeping pills. A half-used cake of soap is stuck to the vanity shelf and an old toothbrush keeps company with a nearly empty can of hairspray, some shaving gear, a tube of toothpaste and a bottle of after-shave. The next room appears to be used as a study. It contains a big untidy desk, a swivel chair and a small filing cabinet. Sarah goes through the desk and finds all the usual stuff...paper, pens, sticky tape, stapler, paper clips and a telex. She checks the telex, nothing stands out. The filing cabinet contains a stack of files in alphabetical order. She painstakingly goes through each one, again nothing of interest. But there's something wrong with this room. At first, Sarah can't quite put her finger on it. Then it comes to her, there's a desk, but no computer. Where is his computer? The room opposite is a similar size but is completely bare apart from some heavy drapes hanging at the window. The lounge room at the front of the house contains a brown velvet lounge suite, six matching chairs and a large mahogany dining table. A cocktail cabinet with rounded glass side panels sits in the far corner of the room. It contains a number of half empty spirit bottles, some dusty cocktail glasses and a cocktail shaker. The room opposite is locked, and there is no sign of a key. Sarah is about to move away when she hears a faint scraping sound coming from the room. She calls out, 'Whose there? Police' There is no reply and the sound ceases. Sarah calls again. Silence.

Outside, Sarah stands in the driveway and looks up at the locked room which is well off the ground. She would need a long ladder to get to the window. She checks the garden shed but there are no ladders.

CHAPTER 16

Tara, Bonnie and Hayley have each enjoyed a shot of bourbon in the office, and are loud and giggly as they ride the elevator down to street level.

'I've had my primer, now I'm ready for the real thing,' shrieks Bonnie.

'It's alright for you, you don't have to drive,' Tara moans.

'You could always catch the train like I do.'

'Can't. I'm being stalked, and trains aren't safe.'

'Don't know how you're coping. If it was me, I'd be on a plane to Alaska,' says Haley.

'You can get stalked in Alaska you know.' The three link arms and walk down Martin Place.

As they enter Chatties Bar and Grill, Bonnie's eyes flit around checking the 'talent'. One guy grabs her attention and she nudges Tara with her elbow. 'There's a cutie.'

Tara looks across. 'Mmm,' she murmurs.

'I'm going for him.'

'All yours,' Tara looks around wondering what she's doing here. Rick is dead. She has to move on, but how? Suddenly the whole scene sickens her. It's false, nothing's real, she's out of her comfort zone, was she ever in one? Her life is one rotten mess. She watches Bonnie and feels embarrassed for her. Bonnie is small and quickly affected by grog. Just the one shot of bourbon at the office intoxicated her. Now she'll do what she does every Thursday night, get totally pissed! In the past, it never worried Tara, but now everything matters, especially the threats to her life.

Bonnie is with the cute guy and Tara and Hayley sip their drinks watching. 'She's smashed already,' Hayley observes.

'So, what's new?'

'See anyone who takes your fancy?'

'Not really interested.'

'Oh Tara, I'm so sorry about Rick.'

'We were over.'

'I know, but...'

'I still love him,' Tara sobs. She buries her head into Hayley's shoulder, her body shaking.

'What on earth happened?'

'He left me. I thought he'd gone back to Elise. Now she's missing and he's dead.'

'It's all too awful. What are you going to do?'

'What can I do? Now I've got some nutter threatening to kill me too.'

'Think it's just a nutter?'

'How in the hell do I know? The cops are patrolling past my place day and night. They must think it's serious.'

'Come and stay with me.'

'God, Hales, you've got a bed sitter. Where would I sleep?'

'I've got a blow-up mattress, that's better than being alone and frightened.'

'Thanks, but look, I've got the cops watching. I'll be okay.'

'If that's what you want.'

'I do. Let's get some food.'

'Hey come on, Thursday night's for having fun.' Hayley drains her glass and motions to the barman.

They find an empty table and make their food orders. Bonnie joins them, flushed and excited. 'His name is Brad, he's hot.'

As soon as she's finished her meal, Bonnie wanders back to Brad and his group.

A tall young man approaches their table. His attention is focused on Hayley. Tara gets the message. 'Look Hales, I think I'll call it a night. If I have another drink, I won't be fit to drive.'

'You're sure?'

'See you tomorrow.' Tara steps out onto George Street and walks quickly to Martin Place. The street is well lit and she takes comfort in the ubiquitous buskers and their intoxicated admirers. The Martin Place Christmas tree is flashing its brilliant kaleidoscope of colours and there's a feeling of goodwill in the air now that the city is out of Covid-19 lockdown.

The basement car park, by contrast, is dark and shadowy. There are only a few cars remaining, all well-spaced from each other. The eerie shadows close in, and Tara suddenly breaks out in a cold sweat. Fear and panic send rushes of adrenalin as she darts to her car. Safe inside, she locks the doors and breathes a sigh of relief. She fumbles in her bag for a tissue and dabs at her moist face. The nearby elevator opens with a creak and two people tumble out. As they walk unsteadily toward their car they talk and laugh loudly. They wear party hats, and colourful streamers hang around their shoulders. *Weeks to Christmas and the parties have already started. What sort of ghastly Christmas will I have?* Tara thinks as she puts the car into motion.

Back in the neon-lit world, she turns on the radio. Triple J is playing a lively tune and she taps at the steering wheel in time with the music. The traffic is normal for this time of night and luckily free of random breath test patrols. Tara's thoughts return to the threatening notes. Who could have sent them? She has no enemies, or has she? Elise probably hates her, but now Elise is missing. Is it Elise making the threats? Where is she? And Travis probably hates her too, maybe he's the one. Rick is dead, murdered, who killed him? Oh, my darling Rick. Tears run down Tara's cheeks as she thinks about Rick, and the day she met him...

She and Travis were on their third drink in the local pub when Rick walked in. He slapped Travis on the back. 'Hey, Trav!!'

'Hey mate, where've you been?' Travis jumped up and they shook hands.

'I've just got back from a backpacking trip around Oz.'

'Tara, meet my best mate. Rick Ballantyne.'

Her eyes nearly popped out. 'What movie set did you just walk off?' she quipped.

Rick grinned widely showing two rows of perfectly shaped white teeth. 'My mate Travis always did have good taste in chicks.'

She was immediately interested. Her relationship with Travis had been very casual, and although Travis was always looking for it, there had been no intimacy. But now, with this gorgeous hunk around, seeing more of Travis could mean seeing more of Mr Wonderful.

She felt Rick was interested, but her relationship with his best mate was holding him back. He also had a girlfriend, a dreary girl called Sienna. Tara worked on Rick at every opportunity, using her glib wit and sexy flirting. She felt she was almost there when Elise appeared on the scene. Elise was as beautiful as Rick was handsome. But although Elise was naive and unworldly, it was obvious she had been blown away by Rick and was sticking to him like glue. Who could blame her? Elise was a big hitch in Tara's plans, but she decided to hang in there. It meant her relationship with Travis would have to improve if she wanted to stay with the group. When he asked her to move in with him, she accepted. Then things started getting really awkward. She lost her job at the local TAB and wasn't helping Travis with rent or food. Although Travis hadn't complained, she had no money for the cosmetics and clothes she loved to splash on. She moaned loudly and Elise responded.

'Tara, one of the clerks in the firm has just resigned. She's having a baby. I could put in a word for you.'

'That would be awesome, thanks.'

Elise got her the job and they travelled together to and from work in Elise's brand-new car. Their relationship bonded further when they joined in with Bonnie and Hayley on their Thursday night "rages".

She realised she'd have to move quickly to calm the waters when Elise caught her fondling Rick at the bike racing night. This was not the time to have a big fallout with the group. Her mind was working frantically. She needed to get Elise back on side. Maybe at the same time, she could gain ground with Rick.

'When are you getting your tats Elise?'

*

She steered Elise to the tattooist on the outskirts of Croydon.

'My parents will kill me.' Elise grizzled.

'Don't be a wuss.'

'It's alright for you, you don't live with yours. You hardly *ever see them.'*

'You can't let them rule you forever. You're nineteen. You're old enough to vote, old enough to go to war, old enough to do your own thing.'

The shop was cool and clean. They were greeted by the proprietor Serge, a big muscular man wearing only a pair of faded tatty jeans. He was so covered in tattoos it was hard to tell his age. Snakes and fire-spitting dragons wove their way over his body and head... a moving kaleidoscope of brilliant colours.

'Hi Serge,' she greeted the tattooist with a kiss. Elise had trouble looking at the man, much less kissing him.

'Hi beautiful, how's Sybil?'

Tara bent over pulled down her panties and displayed a snake tattooed across both cheeks, 'still hissing,' she laughed.

'Beautiful,' he laughed. 'What can I do for you this time?'

'Not me, my friend here. Serge this is Elise.'

The man picked up Elise's hand in his coloured claw, and to Elise's horror, kissed it.

'First question, where?' he grinned showing crooked yellow teeth.

'Somewhere not too noticeable.'

Serge winked at her, 'a little virgin.'

'I am not.'

'I meant in the tattoo department.'

'I'll have one on my foot.'

Tara burst out laughing. 'Elise, you're priceless.'

'No worry princess. We start with the foot. Then you get addicted and come back for more.'

'Now, what you like? See my pictures on the wall? Anything you like. Or just look at Serge and pick something.'

He spread his arms out displaying his colourful body.

Elise wandered around the room looking. There were dozens of photographs, all displaying tattoos in various designs on various body parts.

'Have the spider and his web. I nearly had that one instead of Sybil,' Tara suggested.

'Too much for the foot,' advised Serge.

'I'll have the rose.'

'Good start. Over here my little darling and we get to work. You know my price?'

'She knows.'

It was more than a month before Elise's parents found out about the rose. By then she had a spider on her shoulder.

'Mother knows about the tats. She's raving like a lunatic.'

'What did she say?

'Just what I expected: How can you deface your beautiful body? It's a sacrilege, blah, blah, blah.'

All through summer, the six met every Sunday at the beach. The boys invariably yakked on about football, cars, beer and bikes, while the girls discussed makeup, fashions and films.

Rick stretched out on his towel, cushioned his head under his hands, and with closed eyes said: 'If there's anything on this earth I'd kill for, it's a Harley.'

'What's so good about a Harley?' Courtney asked rubbing sunscreen over her shoulders.

'What a dumb question. It's the king of bikes.'

'Well, if you're that infatuated, why don't you just go out and buy one?' Courtney asked.

'Because dummy, they cost a lot of money, money I don't have.'

Soon after this, Elise approached her. 'Tara, you've

often said how much you love my car. Would you like to buy it? I'll sell it for well below value.'

'I'd love it sweetie, but you don't know what my bank balance looks like.'

'You're earning good money now.'

'But nothing saved. Maybe Travis will give me a loan.'

She got the loan from Travis and Elise sold her the car. Elise told her what transpired when she gave Rick the bike.

'I'm giving you an early birthday present,' Elise cooed to Rick. 'It's waiting for you in an auto yard in Parramatta.' Elise had done her homework. She'd contacted one of the leading Harley-Davidson outlets and had bought the best model she could afford.

Rick was almost speechless, 'Oh babe.'

When Elise bought Rick that fucking bike, Tara felt all the odds were stacked against her. How could she compete with that?

But Rick was seeing things in Elise that disturbed him. Her occasional erratic behaviour started almost immediately after the ill-fated rock concert. Elise would go for months being her old self. Then she would break out in patches of mindless behaviour. She would be illogical, tearful, argumentative, and plain weird.

Tara knew Rick was becoming disenchanted. She waited her time. Finally, Rick confided in her. 'Elise's driving me nuts, she's off her tree.'

'What are you going to do?'

'It's going to be hard, but I'm going to end it.'

'You know, I've always fancied you.'

Rick grinned, 'I've noticed.'

'I'm about to give Travis the flick.'

'I thought you guys were set in concrete.'

'Set in fairy floss, more like. I've never loved Travis.'

'Why have you stuck with him so long?'

'Why do you think?' she grinned, 'to be near you, silly.'

'The guy's my best mate. I couldn't white-ant him.'

'I'm leaving Travis, regardless of what you do.'

'Does he know?'

'Not yet. 'I'll be looking for a flat. When I've got one, then I'll tell him. I can make you happy Rick, just call and I'll come.'

And that's what happened. Rick finished with Elise and moved in with her. The aftermath was traumatic. Elise constantly phoned begging Rick to return to her. In desperation, he changed his number.

Tara recalls the day Elise came to their flat. It was a Sunday in early summer, and they had slept in. The knock on the door had sent them scuttling for clothes.

'It's probably Emmet,' said Rick, but it wasn't Emmet. Elise stood on their doorstep smiling weirdly. 'I've got early Xmas presents, for both of you.' She walked into the living room, leaving them standing at the door, open mouthed and wide eyed.

Elise was pulling packages out of her shopping bag. They were wrapped in bright Xmas paper.

'This is ridiculous, Elise, we can't take presents from you.'

'Of course, you can. And you can offer me a drink, Vodka please.' Elise fell into a chair and threw the packages, one at a time at Rick. Taken by surprise, he managed to catch the first but miss the second.

'You can have the bike back, Elise. I've been meaning to get it to you.'

'What would I do with a big bike like that? No Rick, it's yours, keep it. And every time you ride it, think of me. Now, what about that drink Tara? I'm waiting.'

Tara looked at her watch. 'It's a bit early, isn't it?'

'Not when we're celebrating early Christmas.'

Tara went to the kitchen splashed a good measure of vodka into a glass and plopped in a couple of chunky ice blocks. Agitated and unnerved, she returned to the living room and handed the glass to Elise.'

'Thanks, bottoms up.' Elise swallowed the entire glass without a break. 'I'll have another, bring the bottle.' Elise's voice was harsh. 'Get me another drink, and then open your presents.' Elise threw two packages at her. Both fell to the floor. Slowly she bent down and retrieved them staring all the time at Elise's manic face.

'Open them', shouted Elise. Reluctantly she tore at the paper. A pile of gaudy g/string underwear tumbled out. Rick turned pale and left the room. He returned with the bottle of vodka and placed it on the small table beside Elise.

'Open yours, Rick,' Elise ordered as she poured vodka into her glass.

Rick reluctantly pulled at the paper. Two male g/strings and a huge packet of condoms fell to the floor.

Elise broke into hysterical laughter. 'Just what I need, you're supposed to say.' She stared at them with wild, glaring eyes. 'Be polite, say it,'. She downed the drink and poured another.

'Elise, let me drive you home,' Rick pleaded.

'I can find my own way, thank you very much.' She cast her eyes around the room, taking in the cheap furniture and furnishings. 'What a dump, couldn't you do better?'

'I think you should go, and take your presents with you.' Tara snapped.

'What an ungrateful slut you are Tara.' Elise stood shakily. She planted a kiss on Rick's unyielding lips and staggered out of the house, slamming the door behind her.

Missing In Red

Travis wasn't quite so easy to get rid of. He came around shouting and yelling a week or so later.

'I want my thirty thousand now and while you're at it, you can cough up with my iPad and my camera.'

'Trav, I'll pay you the money. It's just I've had so many big expenses lately.'

'Yeah, like your tattoos and your fancy clothes. It's two months since you've paid me anything. I'll take the car.'

There was a lot of pushing and shoving after that, and Rick threw him out.

A letter of demand came from Travis' solicitor. She ignored it. Nothing happened.

*

It's nearly one when Tara runs the car into the garage. Her reminiscing has been painful. The more she considers the facts, the more confused she becomes. Elise was psychotic and totally off her head when Rick dumped her. It's probably Elise threatening her now, but then again, Travis was raving like a madman about his money. Maybe it's Travis.

She gathers her handbag from the passenger seat and is about to unlock her door when a noise from behind sends adrenalin flooding her body. In that instant, a shining metal strip drops in front of her face and settles at her neck. The wire gouges into her throat, hard, tight and cutting. Her hands fly upward trying to grab the wire and pull it free, but the thing is slitting her throat, deeper and deeper. It slashes into her windpipe. Her eyes bulge and her muffled scream becomes a ghastly gurgle as her mouth fills with blood.

A few moments later a shadowy hooded figure hurries down the dark street. As the figure turns the corner, a police patrol car slowly approaches Tara Gresham's house.

*

Ellington is woken from a dreamless sleep by the funky

tune on his mobile.   He glares at the clock. 'Fuck! Four o'clock.' He grabs the phone. 'Ellington,' he growls.

The voice on the other end is unfamiliar. At first Ellington thinks it's a hoax. 'This is Sergeant Alberghetti from Summer Hill police. That girl we were keeping an eye on in Stewart Street, she's been murdered.'

'You guys were supposed to be watching her,' Ellington groans.

'The patrol car was passing her house regularly. She hadn't come home and the officers had no idea where she was, but when they made their regular check just after one, they noticed the garage door open.   They investigated and there she was in her car, dead, throat cut.'

'Shit.' Ellington growls, forensics there yet?'

'Yeah.'

'Need me?'

'You can't do anything. As you requested the patrols, I thought I should let you know.'

'Thanks. I'll get there soon.'

Ellington's on his way by five thirty. He's been awake since the police call and feels like shit. Dawn is breaking and the pearly grey sky is gradually lightening as he weaves through the early morning traffic. Smoke is still blanketing the city, and the weather forecast promises yet another hot day.

The small duplex is cordoned off with police tape, and a middle-aged cop guards the front driveway. Ellington shows his badge and enters the garage. The forensic personnel are still there, one has his head in the boot and the other is in the back seat.

'What have you found?'

The man at the boot straightens up and looks squarely at Ellington. 'The victim's carotid artery was slashed. Death was pretty quick. There was no sign of a struggle, the killer struck from behind.'

Ellington opens the front driver's door. Heavy blood stains have seeped into the headrest and two thick lines run from it, forming a pool on the seat.

A female voice calls from the back seat: 'I might have something here.' Ivana Mirrakoff holds up a few threads of grey cotton, 'stuck with blood to the back of the seat,' she adds.

'When did they take the body?'

'Just before you got here.'

'I'll need the results of the autopsy along with anything else you might pick up in the car. You have my contact number?'

'I have indeed,' Ivana manages a faint smile.

*

'Tara Gresham was murdered last night,' Ellington talks into his hands-free phone.

Sarah whistles 'Jesus, where, how?'

'In her garage...garrotted.'

'That's awful.'

'I'm on my way to the Seymours. I'll see you at the station in an hour or two.'

'How did you get on with the Gallego case?'

'Murray's making an arrest today. Sorry I didn't get to you at Summer Hill yesterday. How did you go with Brown?'

'I followed him home at midday. I think he just went there for lunch, but after he left, I broke in and took a look around.'

'You what?'

'You heard.'

'Constable, I will pretend I didn't hear you say that.'

'Why? You're the one suspecting Brown, I was just following orders.'

'I never ordered you to break into his house.'

'Well, I found something.'

'What?'

'There's a room in the house that's locked. I think someone's imprisoned in that room. Can we get a warrant?'

'I doubt it, there's really no evidence to show cause.'

'A tall ladder then?'

'Why not just knock on his door when he's home?'

,

CHAPTER 17

Janet Seymour looks gaunt and pale her eyes are watery and red-rimmed. She seems to have aged ten years since Ellington last saw her.

'What can I do for you this time Detective?'

'There's been another murder. May I come in?'

She stands aside and Ellington enters. 'Another? I didn't know anyone had been murdered.'

'We're fairly certain Richard Ballantyne was pushed under that train.'

'Well, that's the first I've heard.' She wanders into the lounge room and Ellington follows.

'Who this time?' She drops heavily onto a lounge chair.

'Tara Gresham.'

'Oh.'

'You don't seem concerned.'

'Why should I? What she did to Elise was deplorable.'

'We are inclined to believe both murders are connected with Elise's disappearance.'

Janet Seymour glares at Ellington her voice sharp and taunting, 'and what *about* Elise's disappearance? What have you been doing? She's been missing a fortnight and you've come up with nothing!'

'We've spent every day trying to find her. We've

interviewed a lot of people. We've been to Canberra and up to Sea Haven.'

'Sea Haven?'

'A girl resembling Elise was seen there. Have you any reason to believe that Elise might be at Sea Haven?'

'I don't even know where it is.'

'A small seaside village up the coast.'

'And what came out of that?'

'We're still making inquiries. Right now, we have three persons of interest: Gregory Allenby, Travis Lockhart and Nathan Brown, the chemist.'

'I think Elise has been abducted and I don't think either the pastor or Mr Brown could be involved.'

'Why not?'

'They're still around. Brown is in his shop every day and Allenby is at the parsonage. If either of them had Elise, they wouldn't be hanging around here, would they? As for Travis Lockhart, I don't really know the man. I only met him a few times.'

Ellington walks to the window and looks out. 'It's very likely the rape has something to do with Elise's disappearance.'

David Seymour appears in the doorway. 'Detective, we are living a nightmare. If Elise isn't found soon, I think we will both........' Seymour doesn't finish his sentence, but closes his eyes and shakes his head.

'I think there might still be a clue in Elise's bedroom. I'd like to take another look.'

Janet Seymour's expression turns grim. 'Why? You've been there twice already.'

'I think it's important.'

'Very well, you know where it is.' She turns her head and faces away from him.

Missing In Red

The room envelops Ellington in its haunting beauty and fairy tale atmosphere. The same weird feeling he had before, takes hold of him. He opens the wardrobe and surveys the rows of pretty dresses and spotless shoes. There amidst the sandals and slippers is a pair of joggers. Why had Elise not worn her joggers that day? Why had she chosen to walk in her high heels? Would that be because she was expecting to meet someone, someone in a car, someone she knew? He checks through the books on the shelf and then turns his attention to the pile of records.   He feels an intimate connection with the girl. He has read her diary, touched her clothes, he knows her taste in books and music. He has never met her but she is so real to him. He desperately wants to find her alive. He picks up the pile of records. Ironically, there's one of Duke Ellington.   He puts it down and picks up another...Nat King Cole. He sets in on the turntable and sits on the bed. The dulcet tones of the long dead singer soothe his tired brain. His head falls on the pillow, and he closes his eyes, listening. *"They tried to tell us we're too young, too young to really be in love. They say that love's the word, the word we've only heard but can't begin to know the meaning of. And yet'....* a noise at the door causes Ellington to snap out of his reverie and raise his head. Through dazed eyes, he sees a beautiful young woman dressed in a slim fitting red dress. She closes the door behind her. Ellington's brain feels as if it's about to explode. 'Elise, you're safe!' he whispers.

'You're Luke. Mother told me you were here.'

'Where have you been?' Ellington sits up.

'It's a long story and I'm terribly tired. '

She walks to the other side of the bed and sits. Her nearness overcomes him with its intoxicating fragrance of violets and roses.

'You needn't give me a formal statement right now. But

do you feel well enough to tell me where you've been and what's been happening to you? Two people have been murdered. Those murders are somehow connected with you.'

She raises her eyebrows and stares widely at Ellington through sapphire blue eyes.

'You were intricately involved with both victims and you had a very emotional discussion with Ballantyne only a few days before he was murdered, the day before you disappeared.'

'You don't think I killed him? I loved him. When I learned that Rick had died, I was devastated.'

'Did you know Tara Gresham was also murdered?'

'I saw it on the television.'

'I read your diary, someone raped you. Was it Allenby?'

She gives a little laugh. 'You cracked my code!'

'Not me, but someone in the department.'

'So, it's public knowledge.'

'Not at all.'

'Not yet,' she says cynically. 'But undoubtedly it will all come out eventually.'

'Was it Allenby?'

'Yes,' she whispers.

'Where have you been?'

'I was abducted by Gregory Allenby.'

'Tell me.'

Elise sighs and her head sinks back onto the propped-up pillow. 'You read my diary. You must know that I didn't particularly like Gregory when I first met him. I thought he was sly, but everyone else, including my parents, thought he was God's gift to the human race.

He begged me to help him write his sermons. I offered to email suggestions. That wasn't good enough, he insisted I come over. He would cook dinner and ply me with wine.' She takes a deep breath. A slight smile creates a dimple on each side of her lovely mouth. 'I pretended I was unaware of the advances he was making. I always managed to keep him at arm's length. Then that last night, that Tuesday night, he raped me. It was ghastly.' She puts her hand to her forehead. 'Later that night Tara phoned. She left a nasty message telling me that she and Rick were through. I thought Rick would come back to me. That helped ease the pain of the rape, but of course, I was wrong,' she sobs. Ellington takes the hand by her side and gently squeezes it. 'If it's too painful....'

'No, I want to tell it all.' She takes a deep breath. 'I met Rick the next morning and he told me I was not a part of his future. I felt like dying all that day, but that night I decided I had to get on with my life. On Thursday I was on my way to the shop when Gregory pulled up alongside me. He pleaded with me to forgive him. He was crying. He said that if I wanted to lay charges, he would drive me to the police there and then. I told him I wouldn't lay charges. He thanked me and offered to drive me to work. Silly me, I felt sorry for him and accepted. Can you believe that? I got into his car. Next thing I know, he's doing a U-turn. '*Where are you going*?' I yelled. He looked at me weirdly, and I could tell from his expression he was not taking me to work. I got out my mobile. He grabbed it from me and threw it out the window. Then he drove to a block of units in a back street in Ashfield. He parked in the underground car park, pulled me out of the car, and pushed me into the elevator. He imprisoned me in an apartment on the top floor and that's where I've been all this time.' Elise turns her head and looks sadly at Ellington. 'He brought me meals twice every day and raped me every night. When I learned that Rick was dead, I wanted to die too. I loved him so much.'

'How did you get away?'

Missing In Red

'The only window in the room was up near the ceiling, long and narrow, the same in the ensuite. I could never get out of either, and the unit was three floors up. But there was a rope mat in the bedroom. I spent every minute of my time unravelling that mat. In the end, I had a long ball and I set up a trip rope. When Gregory came in with my breakfast, I stood against the wall, behind the door. He walked straight into the rope and fell. I tore out of there and took the stairs. Gregory was getting out of the lift just as I was leaving the building. I rushed out into the street, stood in the middle of the road, and waved down a bus. I told the driver I'd been abducted and begged for help. He turned the bus around and took me to Ashfield police station. The sergeant there took my statement and drove me here.' She puts her hand over her eyes. 'I saw you interviewed on television. I knew you were looking for me.' She puts her hand on Luke's. 'Now I want to sleep.' She kicks off her black shoes, lifts her feet onto the bed and closes her eyes. Ellington sees a tiny tear slide down her cheek. His heart melts, the girl has been through emotional torture. He wipes the tear with his finger. 'You'll be okay', he promises.

'Will I? Will I? I feel so lonely and so cold. Hold me Luke'. She moves closer to him and he smells violets in her hair. A sudden noise on the far side of the room startles him. Janet Seymour stands in the doorway, glaring. 'How dare you lie on my daughter's bed,' she shrieks.

'But Elise,' he whispers. He turns his head towards Elise. She's gone. She was never there.

*

By the time he arrives at the station, Ellington is in a depressed mood. The day not even half gone has been traumatic.

Sarah bales him up as he enters the busy room.

'What's happening?'

'I'm waiting on forensic for results of the autopsy. There doesn't appear to be any clues so far, apart from a few strands of grey cotton.'

'The cloaked assassin?'

'Could well be.' He looks at his watch. 'Maybe now would be a good time to have another talk with chemist Brown...at his house.'

It's just after one. Nathan Brown arrives on cue and drives into his property unaware of the car parked nearby. Ellington and Sarah wait a few minutes before going to the front door.

'How can I help you?' Surprise mingles with tension.

'Can we come in?'

Brown hesitantly steps aside and ushers them into the lounge room. As they pass the locked door, Sarah swivels her eyes and surreptitiously points a finger. Ellington gets the message and nods.

With a wave of his hand, Brown indicates the lounge. He sits on a straight-backed dining chair. Ellington and Sarah remain standing.

'We're still no closer to finding Elise Seymour, and we have reason to believe you're not telling us everything.'

'I've told you everything I know.'

'Did Elise Seymour ever come to this house?'

'Never,' he snaps.

'You were mentioned in her diary in an unfavourable way. That can't be ignored. Please don't leave the area without advising us.'

Ellington strides out. Pretending disorientation, he walks to the locked door and turns the knob.

'This way sergeant.' Brown's voice is charged with panic.

'Sorry Mr Brown, someone in that room? I think I just

heard something.'

'No one there, it's just my office, I keep it locked. There are some important papers in that room.'

'I heard something too,' chips in Sarah.

'You will have to give me the key, sir.'

'I tell you, there's nothing in there.'

'The key please.'

Brown shuffles back to the lounge room and extracts a key from under the cocktail cabinet. He grudgingly hands it to Ellington.

The door opens and a foul smell hits them. In the far corner of the room is a pile of straw, sitting on it is a small goat.

Ellington and Sarah exchange surprised glances.

'Nothing?' Ellington's tone reeks of sarcasm.

'Well, she's just my pet. I keep her indoors for her safety. Next door's dogs once jumped the fence and thank God I was home.'

Ellington moves to the untidy desk. A computer sits in the centre surrounded by piles of DVDs and coloured photographs. Ellington sifts through them and squaring his attention at Brown, says: 'You like a bit of porn, I see.'

'They're not mine, they belong to a friend.'

Sarah joins Ellington at the desk and looks at the sordid pile. She squints with repulsion at the explicit photos.

'They're disgusting.'

'There's no law,' Brown mutters.

'Depends what you're doing with them.' Sarah says sharply. She walks to the goat which hasn't moved. 'Poor little creature. You should be out in the field with your mates.' It looks at her with soulful eyes and baas.

On the journey back to the Station, Sarah breaks the silence that had settled on them. 'What's with the goat?'

Missing In Red

'I hate to think.' Ellington mutters. The events of the long day are crowding in on him and all he wants now is to get home and sleep.

CHAPTER 18

With a wave of his hand, Chief Inspector Bellamy summons Ellington to his office.

'Some disturbing news, Campbell's out, and two officers are dead.'

Ellington's eyes screw up as if warding off intolerable glare. 'What?'

'Escaped, just got word.'

Ellington's squint hasn't relaxed, now his jaw is clenching.

'How?'

Bellamy sits heavily. 'He was being transported to hospital for a gall bladder operation. A patrol car waved them down, only it was a fake and the officer was a fake. He shot the two police at close range. Campbell was in the back of the wagon with another prison officer.'

'How could it happen?'

'The officer driving had been reporting their progress on his phone. He mentioned a patrol car up ahead blocking the road, said a uniformed police officer was approaching. The conversation ended abruptly with the sound of two shots being fired. By the time our blokes got there, Campbell, the prison officer and the phony cop were gone.'

'Who was the prison officer?'

'A young bloke, been working in the gaol for seven years, name's Mohammed Mahmoud. Apparently never gave a day's trouble. His parents are distraught.'

'Where do they live?'

'Lakemba. There's a younger brother.'

'How would Campbell's accomplice know the exact time and place?'

'Exactly, that's why it looks like an inside informer.'

'Like Mahmoud, for instance?

Bellamy shrugs and shakes his head. 'The route they were taking was being closely monitored. The fake car must have appeared just minutes or maybe even seconds before the wagon arrived. It was precision timing.'

'Witnesses?'

'Stacks, but none useful. Immediately the media got hold of the incident, people started phoning in. Several motorists passed the two police vehicles, but no one reported anything. To them, it just looked like police going about their business. A few people even saw the two uniformed people getting into the phony car with the handcuffed prisoner. It was only after the fake car left the scene that the police wagon attracted closer attention. One motorist glanced in the wagon's window as he passed and realised there was something wrong. By then our own people were arriving at the scene.'

'How did they get away?

'The holdup was near a highway exit. They dumped the car a few kilometres along. They obviously had another car waiting. Unfortunately, in *that* location there were no witnesses.'

'How urgent is Campbell's operation?'

'Very, I'm told. He'll be in a lot of pain when his meds wear off, and if the problem isn't fixed, he could die.'

'So, he'll need medical attention.'

'Correct. The underworld has a few blokes they use for these purposes. The most likely is a local guy been operating for decades. Name's Alexander Petrovic. He was de-registered back in the seventies, did time for manslaughter, professional negligence.'

'Know where he is?'

'Yes, and we're watching him. So far nothing, but he's a clever bastard, he'll know he's been watched.'

'So, it would appear that Mohammed Mahmoud is either the informer or a hostage.'

'Or dead.' Bellamy rubs his palm across his forehead. 'When you were hunting him down, you must have got to know some of Campbell's haunts and habits. Got any ideas?'

'He won't go near any of his old haunts. He's too smart for that.' Ellington sits opposite Bellamy. 'If he's in need of medical treatment, I reckon that'll be his first move.' Ellington looks squarely at Bellamy. 'Campbell threatened me in court. I'd like to be involved in this one.'

'How's the Seymour thing going?'

'I've got both Lockhart and Allenby under surveillance.'

'And?'

'Lockhart seems to be leading a normal life. Allenby however regularly visits a prostitute in Ashfield.'

'Could the lady be hiding the girl or perhaps a body?'

'She's been known to police for a long time. She's registered, and I'm pretty sure she would steer well clear of abduction or murder.' Ellington eyeballs his chief. 'I think when Campbell's recovered, he'll come after me. That's why you've got to let me in on this.'

'It's important that Petrovic's surveillance continues. I've got a team on that.' Bellamy mutters.

'Have you talked with Goulburn?'

219

'We've already been there, but I'm good if you think talking to them again would be worthwhile.' Bellamy fixes Ellington with a stern stare. 'But first, talk to Mahmoud's family.'

*

The house is a small weatherboard in central Lakemba. A short middle-aged woman in an ankle length dress peers at him through dark-framed glasses.' Mrs Mahmoud?' The woman nods. 'I'm Detective Sergeant Ellington, South Sydney Police. I'm investigating Mohammed's disappearance. May I come in?'

The woman opens the door and wordlessly indicates for him to enter. The room is dark and cluttered. A sagging lounge takes up half a wall along with a battered ill matching single armchair. A coffee table laden with magazines sits in the middle of the room and a cane sofa stands against another wall. A small cat lies sleeping beneath the coffee table. There is a strange odour hanging in the air, a combination of spicy cooking, mustiness and damp clothing.

A short thin man appears from the hallway. His face has sunken through lack of teeth and his hair and moustache are heavily streaked with grey. It's difficult for Ellington to estimate his age. He guesses somewhere between fifty and sixty.

'You here about Mohammed?'

'Yes.'

The woman leaves the room much to Ellington's consternation. He needs to talk with her too. The man points to the armchair and sits opposite on the cane lounge.

'When did you last see Mohammed?

'Three weeks ago. He came for weekend.'

'Did he seem worried, anxious?'

The man exudes concern. 'We are proud of our Mohammed. He gets good job. He does well, no trouble, ever.'

'That's very good, sir, but I'm trying to find out if other people might have been causing *him* trouble.'

'He said nothing to me.' The man clenches his jaw, and narrows his eyes. 'You must find my boy.'

'We will do our best. I'll need to talk with your younger son. Is he around?'

'Bilal at school.'

The woman enters with a tray. She now wears a scarf that wraps around her head and the lower part of her face. 'Apple tea,' she says putting the tray on the small section of available space on the coffee table. She hands Ellington a cup and then one to her husband.

'Mrs Mahmoud, did Mohammed say anything to you recently about being worried or upset?'

'Mohammed always happy, no upset.'

Ellington sips the hot sweet tea. 'When does Bilal get home?'

The man looks to the ceiling, purses his lips, 'four sometimes four-thirty.'

Ellington consults his watch, it's nearly four. He finishes the tea and rises. 'I'll come back at four-thirty.'

He goes to his car and calls Bellamy. 'The parents aren't giving much away and the young brother's still at school. I'm waiting around for him, shouldn't be long.'

It's nearly four-thirty and there is still no sign of Bilal. Ellington goes back to the house. 'Where do you think Bilal might be?' he asks.

The father shrugs. 'He good boy, maybe he goes to Mosque.'

Ten minutes later Ellington stands to leave. Almost simultaneously, the front door opens. A tall slender youth is framed in the doorway. His dark eyes flash from Ellington to his parents, and then back to Ellington.

'Bilal?' Ellington asks.

'Yeah, who wants to know?' he closes the door behind him.

'Detective Sergeant Ellington, South Sydney Police.' He shows his ID. 'I'm investigating the disappearance of your brother.' The boy looks defiantly at Ellington and says nothing.

'Have you any idea what might have happened to him?'

'My brother's been captured, probably dead.'

'Bilal!' His mother cries. 'Don't say these things.'

'Did Mohammed talk with you about being threatened by anyone?'

'No.'

'Were you surprised when he disappeared?'

'What the fuck's that supposed to mean? Of course, I was surprised.'

'And there's absolutely nothing at all you can tell me that might help me find him?'

'No.' The boy strides off down the hall. Inside his room he punches a number into his mobile and speaks softly, 'A cop came asking questions.'

Inside a double-storied building and squatting on the cement floor, Mohammed Mammoud talks to his brother on the phone. 'What was he asking?'

'About you, where you might be etcetera, etcetera.'

'What did you tell them?'

'Nothing man. What do you think I am?'

'When you come here, just make sure no one's following. Okay?'

'Okay. When should I come?'

'Lay low for a day. Then bring some more food and underwear....and some soap. I've got some tinned food to see me out 'till then. And bring a decent pillow and a sleeping bag.'

*

Ellington's nerves are jangled, and the nightmare has returned with a vengeance. The iron arm grabs him and the knife comes slashing down. His conscious mind takes him back to when the nightmares first started. It was ten years ago, long before he knew of Campbell and long before he became a senior detective. But those nightmares, although different from the ones now assailing him, were also the product of an event that occurred during his policing duties. He recalls the event clearly.

February 2012

He was a rookie cop at the time and stationed in an outer-western Sydney suburb. A call came through that a big shipment of drugs was changing hands. Ten officers were organised to take possession of the drugs and arrest all those involved. What transpired that night was a disaster that had an overwhelming emotional effect on Ellington. His depression deepened, and his short fuse sparked bouts of anger. Nikki complained and they argued constantly.

It came to a head one sultry Sunday morning. The heat hung over the city in a thick, hazy blanket. Nikki had suggested the beach. Ellington shook his head.

'Why, Luke? It's a hot day. I'd like to cool off.'

'You'll get burned.'

'Rubbish, we can take the beach umbrella. We don't have to stay all day, just an hour or two.'

Ellington didn't reply, instead, he turned on the television. Nikki turned it off.

'We don't go anywhere. You won't talk to me. I can't take much more. You bloody- well need help.' She stormed off to the bedroom. Ellington said nothing, and turned the television back on. Nikki drove to the beach, couldn't get the umbrella up, stayed too long and got burned. She blamed Ellington for the pain she suffered in the following days, and the wall of silence grew between them.

It was the final straw when Ellington refused to go to her brother's wedding. 'I don't like him, and I'm not going.'

'It's my family, my parents all my relatives will be there. I've got to go.'

'Then go by yourself.'

'If I go alone, then that's it. I won't be coming back.'

*

The day came and Ellington stuck to his word and refused to go. Nikki stuck to hers too. She packed two big suitcases and threw them into her car. She didn't return, and Ellington didn't go looking for her. They had been together more than a year, and it seemed the relationship was set in concrete. But Ellington's recent mental instability had shattered the concrete into a load of rubble.

The nightmares had not only wrecked his relationship with Nikki, but were also interfering with his work. Chief Inspector Cameron cornered him one morning. 'The de-briefing you received, obviously didn't help. If you want to keep your job, you'll see the Department's chief psychologist.' He handed Ellington a card.

Since living alone, all structure seemed to have left Ellington's life. Most of the time he didn't bother cooking and often ended up with a hunk of cheese and a can of beer for his dinner. Tonight, was no exception, except that the one can of beer had suddenly become three. He turned the psychologist's card over in his hand and wondered how could it come to this? What was wrong with him that he couldn't let things go like the other guys? He wanted to forget that night, but try as he did, he just couldn't. The memories were always there, lurking. He decided to sleep on it and consider the psychologist tomorrow.

Sleep finally came but it was anything but peaceful. He was there again in another dark lane, one with long shapeless shadows and reeking of cheap grog and rotting vegetables. The sky was starless and heavy as black velvet. Ellington's sub-conscious recalled the humidity and the prickling sensation of sweat on his back. He saw the old drunk propped against a wall and Kinnane kicking him, saw the man's shoulders rise, his body quivering a little and then slumping. Ellington wondered why Kinnane kicked him, what was the point? He hadn't time to further consider this because his attention was taken by the yelling coming from inside the house. He heard the shot that shattered the silence, saw Kinnane pull out his pistol. The boy appeared on the landing, the light illuminating his slight body and pale skin.

'*Hands in the air,*' Kinnane yelled. The boy slowly descended the stairs, arms reaching above his head. As he moved off the last step his hand dove into a hip pocket. Simultaneously an explosion ripped through the lane. The boy's eyes widened with surprise as he slowly crumpled down. Ellington rushed over, knelt beside the boy, and felt for a pulse. He saw the red stain widening on the white shirt and reluctantly looked at the boy's face. A wave of emotion flooded his body as his eyes met those of the dead boy...eyes that would be staring at him for months to come.

*

Leading up to the Inquiry, Ellington felt he was in a fishbowl...questions and innuendoes. He tried to avoid Kinnane but the guy seemed to be always hanging around, bringing him cups of coffee and acting all palsy-walsy.

Ellington started to dread the day when he would have to give his evidence and re-live the whole rotten night.

The chief inquisitor was a senior officer…a tall middle-aged woman with raven black hair pulled severely back from her pale square face. Small brown eyes peered from behind dark-rimmed glasses. The jacket of her dark grey suit was undone, showing a plain white shirt beneath. Her voice was loud and officious as she questioned Kinnane.

'Tell the Inquiry what happened the night Jarrod Vicary was killed.' Ellington watched Kinnane's face as he gave his account and answered her questions. He seemed to have adopted an innocent, little boy expression. Even his voice sounded different…soft and sincere. Ellington knew Kinnane had lost it, that he was a hot head and a bully. But now, he was presenting like the Angel Gabriel, giving an embellished account that made him look like a hero protecting all and sundry.

Then it was Ellington's turn. He stammered his statement…all truth. A silence followed that seem to last for ages. At last Chief Inspector Dredge spoke: 'So Constable Ellington…how long have you been a police officer?'

'Two years.'

'In those two years, how many times have you been on an operation such as the one you took part in on the night of…' Dredge quickly consulted her notes. 'December the twentieth, two thousand and eleven?'

'That was the first.'

'Really? What had you been doing in those two years?'

'Traffic duty and desk duty.'

Dredge's small brown eyes were penetrating. 'You have told the Inquiry that you believe Senior Constable Kinnane acted hastily and without thought. Why is that?'

'The deceased was a young man who was not carrying

a weapon. He made no attempt to run away.'

'But Senior Constable Kinnane was not to know the deceased was unarmed. It was a very dark night, no moon, no stars. Isn't that, right?' Dredge stared hard at Ellington. 'As a junior, inexperienced Constable, why do you think you can make such an assessment?'

'It's how I saw it.'

'And what did you see? Not much, I think.' Ellington remained silent. Dredge continued: 'A gun had been fired from inside the house you were guarding, and only seconds later a person emerges from the building. You knew there was a drug exchange going on inside and that dangerous criminals were likely to be involved...right?'

'Yes.'

'And that this stranger was likely to be armed. In fact, it was possible that this person had discharged the firearm inside the house and was trying to escape. Then when he reached into his pocket, don't you think Constable Kinnane acted appropriately in his effort to protect both you and himself?'

'Jarrod...the deceased, was only a kid.'

'How was Constable Kinnane to know that?'

'When he came out onto the landing, he was lit up. There was a light on the landing.'

'I have had that light tested. It is 40 watts. That is extremely feeble wattage, and of little benefit on a dark night. The stairs were in darkness.'

Kinnane got off. The Inquiry found he had been protecting others and himself in the line of duty. Ellington felt sick when he thought of the kid's grieving family. He was their only son, doing well at school, a life ahead wasted.

*

Mary Quinn's house was cool and pleasant. An

overhead fan circulated the air and ruffled the lacy curtains. Incense, mingled with the perfume of cut flowers created a curious but soothing fragrance. She greeted Ellington with a smile and a firm handshake. She wasn't what he expected. He had pictured a department psychologist to be big, mannish. But Mary was small and dainty with soft dark curls framing a cherubic face. She wore a pale-yellow shift and flat sandals.

'Sit down Constable. May I call you Luke?' Her voice soft and low.

'Yes', he murmured. Their two chairs were placed so close together that when he looked into her face, he could see the little flecks of green in her pale blue eyes. She smiled gently. 'Would you like some water?' She nodded towards the jug and glasses sitting on the little three-legged table nearby.

'No thank you.'

Mary joined her hands together and placed them in her lap. 'Now Luke, tell me why you're here.'

'You know why I'm here.'

'Yes, Inspector Cameron told me about your problem, but I want to hear it from you.'

'I'm having nightmares. They're interfering with my work.'

'Tell me about the nightmares. How and when did they begin?'

'They started soon after the...incident.'

'Tell me about the incident.'

Ellington tightened his hands into fists and clenched his jaw. He hated thinking about it but there was no getting out of it now. His words came out slowly, quietly, hesitantly. He kept his eyes cast down looking at his clenched fists.

'There'd been a tip-off. A big haul of drugs was about to change hands. We knew the time, the date and the place.

It was a gambling joint in Smithfield. There were ten of us...no sirens, no blue lights. We parked the cars in the lane at the back of the house. Sergeant McGaw told me and Kinnane to stay in the lane, watch the back door and apprehend anyone trying to get away. Two men were to guard the front entrance while the other six went inside.' Ellington raised his eyes and looked tensely at Mary.

She smiled and nodded encouragingly. 'Go on.'

'After a few minutes, we heard a lot of shouting and yelling coming from inside. Then there was a shot. Kinnane took out his pistol and moved towards the building. I followed him.

Then this kid came out and started down the stairs. Kinnane yelled at him to stop and raise his hands. The kid stopped, raised his hands, and looked at us, real scared. Then he put his hand in his pocket and ....' Ellington gulped as the memories flooded back. 'Kinnane shot him—in the chest.' Ellington rubbed the back of his hand across his eyes. 'There was nothing in the kid's pocket, just his wallet with his ID. He wasn't into drugs, a clean skin, just a kid in the wrong place at the wrong time. He was still at school, scared because his parents would have given him a hiding if they knew he'd been visiting an illegal gambling joint.' Ellington swallowed and stared hard at Mary. ' Kinnane killed him and I did nothing to stop him.'

'Could you have?'

'When I saw the gun, I could have told him to put it away.'

'Was Kinnane your senior?'

'Yes. I was provisional. Kinnane was a senior constable.'

'Then how could you tell him what to do?'

'I dunno.'

'Tell me what happens in your dream.'

'Pretty much what happened in reality, except for one very important thing, Kinnane doesn't shoot the kid. I do! I've shot that kid at least thirty times.'

'You're carrying a lot of guilt Luke, for no good reason.' Mary walked to the window and closed the heavy drapes throwing the room into semi-darkness.

'Lie on the couch. If it would make you feel more comfortable, take off your shoes. I'm going to put some affirmations into your subconscious that I think will help.'

Ellington lay on the couch and closed his eyes. Soft piano music filled the room and the smell of incense seemed to intensify. Mary's calm voice guided him to relax his body, starting at his toes right up to the top of his skull. She then quietly spoke about the shooting. Ellington began drifting into a peaceful semi-conscious state, but all the time he could hear her words. After a while, there was silence, broken only by the soothing music. Then Mary spoke again softly. 'I am going to give you a tape that will help you recover. Every day you will feel a real commitment to play the tape. You will come and see me once a week for the next four weeks. Every day you will feel better, and you will accept that you were in no way responsible for the shooting of that boy. Now on the count of three, you will wake feeling refreshed and renewed. One...two...three.'

Ellington opened his eyes and blinked a few times, regaining focus.

Mary smiled. 'I think we need to do this once a week for the next few weeks. I'll make up the tape and you must play it every day. Pick it up this afternoon.'

'Okay'.

'How do you feel?'

'Fine.'

'Good, same time next week?'
'Sure.'

And so, Ellington did what Mary instructed. He kept his appointments, and every night listened to the tape. Gradually the nightmares stopped. Nikki had gone to live with her sister on the other side of Sydney. He thought of contacting her, but then reminded himself that she had shot through when he needed her most. He had enjoyed her company and liked the sex, but had he really loved her? He wasn't sure just exactly what love was, maybe now would be a good time to make a fresh start.

CHAPTER 19
December 2021

The reminiscing has reminded Ellington that Mary's counselling had completely eradicated the nightmares. There had been none up until the night Campbell attacked him in the quarry. Then the nightmares started again, only these were different and even more distressing than the previous ones. The brief respite he had enjoyed in recent weeks, had convinced him they were gone forever. But since Campbell's escape, they were back with a vengeance bringing the same distress and torment as before. He reaches for his phone and calls Mary Quinn.

*

'Luke, I'm so happy to see you.' Mary extends both hands in greeting. She holds onto Ellington's, and looks deeply into his eyes.
'You were always special to me.'
'Why Mary?'
'You remind me of my son.'
'That would be an incredible compliment, I'm sure.'
'Michael was a wonderful human. He died too young.'
'I'm sorry.'
'We don't always know what we have until we lose it.'
'How do I remind you of Michael?'
'You have the same intensity and the same sense of

justice. Come and tell me what's happening to you.'

Ellington tells her about Campbell and the nightmares.

'You belong to a group of people who not only have vivid dreams but also remember them in fine detail. When the dream is a nightmare, this gift, if you can call it a gift, can be disastrous.' She smiles wanly. 'This one will take longer to fix, I'm afraid. Your nightmare before was caused by your own sense of justice and unsupported guilt. This one, however, is based on reality. There is someone threatening you, someone real. What are you doing to protect yourself?'

Mary's question comes as a surprise.

'I'm being wary.'

'And what if it was a member of the public being threatened?'

'I'd place that person in tight security, might even move them to a new address, guarded of course.' As he says this, a wave of guilt sweeps over him. He didn't do that for Tara Gresham.

'And for your own self, being *wary* is enough?' Mary makes the word sound innocuous.

'I'm a policeman. I'm here to protect people.'

'Policemen *are* people. For starters, I think you should be getting the same sort of protection you'd give to others.' She smiles 'I would hate anything to happen to you.'

'How did Michael die?' he asks.

'Cancer, it's a bugger.'

Ellington shakes his head sadly. They sit in comfortable silence for a few minutes and then Ellington asks: 'are you going to give me some affirmations?'

'I want you to get protection, my affirmations will come later. Promise me you'll do this.'

Ellington comes away shaken. He hadn't thought about police protection and it hadn't been offered by his chief or anyone else.

*

Sarah carries her coffee to Ellington's desk and sits on the spare chair. 'I've heard about Campbell's escape. What's happening?'

'He's still at large.'

'He threatened you, right?'

'In court.'

'Are you concerned?'

He looks at her, battling his emotions. 'Yes,' he murmurs.

'From what I've learned, he's an animal, another Hannibal Lecter. He even eats parts of his victims.'

'Don't rub it in.'

'Are you going to keep up the surveillance on Allenby and Lockhart?'

'Yes, for the time being. I've got Salerno and Pascoe on it.' Ellington fiddles with his mobile. 'I'm driving down to Goulburn tomorrow. I need to talk to the people there about Mahmoud.'

*

Goulburn gaol has been a penitentiary for one hundred and seventy years. Its massive sandstone buildings are home to some of Australia's most dangerous criminals. The grounds are well attended and there is adequate parking. Ellington shows his ID and following directions, parks his car. Although it's summer, there is a crispiness in the air, typical of the Southern Highlands. He deeply inhales the fragrant air as he walks toward the main building.

Warden Richardson wears a sombre expression and speaks in a voice that commands respect. 'Mahmoud only knew about the transportation of Campbell that same morning. Although for two days prior, it was common knowledge Campbell would be facing surgery.'

'What sort of employee is Mahmoud?'

'Obeys the rules, does what he's told.'

'Would you have picked him as an informer?'

'No.'

'Anyone here you might see as an informer?'

'I don't think so, but how can you know?'

'Well, there has to be. The accomplice that held up the wagon knew exactly the route and exactly the time.'

'There's only one route to Goulburn hospital.'

'Maybe so, but the timing was precision. That fake patrol car arrived seconds before the wagon. Do you mind if I talk to some of the other officers, ones that worked closely with Mahmoud?'

'Go ahead.'

The first officer Ellington questions, is a middle-aged ex-policeman named Rafter. The man's restless hands and weird facial expressions lead Ellington to suspect that he has some form of illness. *Why on earth is such a person in charge of prisoners*? he wonders.

'Did Mohammed discuss prisoner Campbell with you at any time?

'No.'

'Did you see Mohammed and Campbell engaged in personal conversation that morning?'

'No.'

And the questions went on. Ellington interviews several more officers. Nothing offered, nothing gained.

Ellington, frustrated, is left with the question: *If Mahmoud isn't guilty, where is he?*

Ellington stands at Bellamy's office door. 'Nothing worthwhile came out of the prison. I wouldn't mind having a talk with Alexander Petrovic.'

'Go for it, but don't forget, he's still under surveillance.'
'Okay if I take Constable Bradley?'
'Fine with me.'

*

Petrovic lives in an impressive home in Kensington. Set on a large block, the house is a reminder of the splendid architecture prevalent in the well-to-do Sydney homes of the mid-twentieth century. A manicured front garden contains a variety of statues and a sprouting fountain. A curving stone staircase sweeps up to a large veranda and an ornate lead-light front door. A dog barks from inside, followed by the sound of light footsteps. The door is opened by a small thin man. His dark beady eyes and hawk-like nose give the impression of a bird of prey. Dressed in a turtle-neck top, designer jeans and expensive leather loafers, he looks more like an artistic movie director, than a convicted criminal. A large black dog on a short leash gives a loud bark. Petrovic frowns and speaking with an East European accent says: 'What now? If this is about the Campbell guy, you've come to the wrong place.'

'Detective Sergeant Ellington.' He shows his identification, 'and Senior Constable Bradley.' Sarah flashes hers. 'And yes, we are here about Campbell. May we come in?'

The man holds up his hands in a defensive pose, purses his lips, and turns inside, leaving them at the door. They follow him and his dog into the cool house. He leads them into a large room featuring expensive furniture, plush carpet and walls adorned with beautiful works of art. A grand piano occupies a large corner section and an ornate bar sits in another. He walks to the bar and pours himself a drink.

'Can't offer one to cops on duty, can I?' He holds up the bottle.

'No, you can't. We have reason to believe you recently treated Clarence Campbell for a gall bladder problem.'

'Don't know where you got that, and there's another thing I don't know: who *is* this Campbell guy?' He takes a long swig of his drink. 'I know you guys are watching me. It's plain as dogs' balls.'

'Do you mind if we take a look around?'

'Got a warrant?'

'No.'

'Didn't think so, the other cops that came knocking didn't either. But I'm feeling in a real good mood right now, so be my guest.' He extends his arms sideways and walks out onto the front veranda. Ellington and Sarah exchange glances. Ellington turns his head in a 'let's go' motion and walks out into the hall. Sarah follows. They search the entire house and find nothing of consequence. They meet Petrovic on the front veranda. 'Happy now?' he asks sarcastically.

'Don't leave the city without advising us,' Ellington says curtly.

As they walk back to the car, a tree load of cicadas sets up a deafening chorus.

'Cicadas are singing, summer is here,' Sarah murmurs.

CHAPTER 20

Fifteen days pass and Ellington's nightmare recurs every night. He hasn't taken Mary Quinn's advice but sleeps with his pistol under the pillow.

'Anything happening with Petrovic?' he asks Bellamy.

'He's still under surveillance, but nothing happening.'

'Surely Campbell will be getting back to him for post-operative care.'

'They use key-hole surgery these days. After-care is minimal and if the operation goes well, the patient is usually back on his feet in a fortnight. And we don't know for sure that Petrovic *is* the surgeon.'

'Campbell could be up and about right now.'

'Exactly, what's the latest in the Seymour case?'

'We seem to have struck a dead end there too. Our surveillance on Lockhart and Allenby is continuing. Neither seems to be departing from his normal habits.'

'Okay, keep with it.' Bellamy struts off.

Sarah walks over. 'I'm off for a drink, like to come?'

Ellington looks at his watch. 'Okay'.

In the bar, they meet at the counter. 'My shout. Beer?' Sarah asks.

'I think I need something stronger. I'll get them.'

'You can get the next lot. This one's on me. So, what is it?'

'Scotch.'

Sarah makes the orders and they carry their drinks to a booth.

'What's going on Luke?'

'Campbell's still at large and no one knows where he is.'

'I've noticed you've been staying back at night.'

'So?'

'So why?

'That's my business.'

'I think it's because you might be frightened of going home.'

'You can think what you like.'

Sarah's expression flattens. She shrugs her shoulders and takes a sip of her drink.

'I'm sorry,' he mumbles.

'It's your life.'

*

Almost immediately Ellington enters his apartment, he knows something is wrong. A chair is out of place and there's a putrid smell. He reaches for his pistol and walks through to the kitchen, then on to the bedroom and into the bathroom. The smell is overpowering and there's blood on the floor. In the shower recess hanging by its tail from the shower rose, is a large black cat. Its dead eyes stare in terror and a wide gash across the throat has almost severed its head.

*

'Was it a break-in?' Sarah asks.

'No. He must have a key.'

'Where would he have got it?'

'The only people with keys are the Strata Manager and

the Real Estate Agent.'

'It'd be worth calling them both, don't you think?'

'I have. Nothing missing from either. I'm having the locks changed and I'm going to a locksmith way-way away.'

'Why the cat? If he wanted to kill you, why didn't he hide in the apartment and wait for you?'

'He intends killing me but he wants to see me squirm.'

'I think you should get out of that place. Do you have friends, relatives to stay with?'

'I would never put friends or family in danger.'

'Then move to a motel or something.'

'He'd find me.'

'Aren't you scared?'

Ellington looks at her intently, his eyes narrow. 'Indeed, I am.'

'Luke, I live alone and there's a spare room. Campbell won't know anything about me, and if he did, he'd have to deal with two of us.'

Ellington puts his hand on Sarah's. 'It's tempting, but I still think I'd be putting you in danger.'

'We'll face it together. Please.'

Ellington shakes his head. 'Not yet.'

*

Ellington spends the following day checking reported sightings of Elise Seymour and the cloaked figure. They are time consuming and unproductive. Most turn out to be hoaxes.

He eats alone at the local Chinese, and heads on home at nine.

When he opens the door, his body stiffens. There's that smell again. He reaches for his pistol and moves stealthily into the apartment and through to the ensuite. He almost gags at the sight. Dripping blood all over his shower recess and covered in maggots, is another dead cat hanging by its tail.

Ellington spends the night sitting in the living room with his pistol in his lap.

*

Sarah knows as soon as she sees Ellington there's something wrong.

'What's happened?'

'He came again last night, so much for changing the locks. He must have a master key.'

'You can't stay there. My offer's still on.'

*

Ellington follows Sarah home and parks in the spare space next to her car.

'Got a double park, I see.'

'It costs extra but it's good for storing junk.'

'I don't see any junk.'

'Got rid of it when I thought you'd be coming.'

Ellington feels comfortable in Sarah's bright little apartment. She heats up two frozen dinners and they watch the television news while they eat. There's a brief segment on the Gresham murder but nothing more on the disappearance of Elise Seymour.

'You'd think with Elise Seymour being the daughter of a politician, there'd be more coverage.'

Ellington shrugs. 'Maybe it's not newsworthy enough.'

Ellington takes a long time to get to sleep and when he does, the dreaded nightmare invades his subconscious. He wakes in a sweat at five and stays that way until he hears Sarah moving around in the kitchen. She's wearing a short flimsy dress, and her honey-coloured hair falls loosely around her shoulders. She turns and smiles. 'Hi, sleep okay?'

'For a while.'

'Cereal, toast, eggs, bacon, fruit, coffee?'

'Fruit and coffee will be fine.'

He watches as Sarah flits around the kitchen organising the fruit and coffee. She looks so different out of uniform …pretty and fragile.

'We might as well go in one car, you can leave yours here,' she chirps.

'Okay.'

They drive in silence for a few kilometres before Sarah says: 'I can almost hear your brain ticking. What are you planning for today?'

'I can't stop thinking of Bilal Mahmoud. He was very defensive when I questioned him. I think he knows something.'

Ellington taps on Inspector Bellamy's office door.

'Come in,' Bellamy shouts.

'Has Bilal Mahmoud been put under surveillance?'

'Should he?'

'I think it would be a good idea. I'd like to volunteer.'

'Fine with me.'

'Okay if I take Bradley?'

'Go ahead.'

They drive to Lakemba in Sarah's car. Mrs Mahmoud half opens the door and stares warily at them.

'I'm sorry to bother you again, but I would like to know which school Bilal attends.'

'Why you want our Bilal?'

'He's not in trouble. We just want to have another word with him.'

'Bilal goes to the public high school.'

'The local school?'

The woman nods.

'Is he at school today?'

She nods again and closes the door. Ellington re-joins

Sarah who has stayed in the car. The local high school is less than a kilometre from the house.

They park near the open double gates and walk along a wide concrete area to the first of four buildings. Following signs and arrows, they come to an office with *Administration* written in gold letters on the door. They knock and enter. The room is large with two desks, several filing cabinets and a long counter cluttered with cups, a coffee maker and plastic canisters. One desk is vacant and a mousy haired woman working on her computer sits at the other. A frosted door marked *Private* is on the far wall. She looks up as they enter: 'Can I help you?'

Ellington and Sarah show their IDs. Ellington speaks: 'Detective Sergeant Ellington and Senior Constable Bradley. We would like to talk with the person in charge...the headmaster?'

'Do you have an appointment?'

'Afraid not.'

'Mr Crawford might be available.' She crosses to the frosted door and knocks.

'Come in,' calls a deep male voice. The woman reappears after a few minutes. She stands by the door holding it open. 'Mr Crawford can see you.'

Crawford's office is small and stuffy. He half rises with an open hand stretched across his desk. He remembers the current Covid-19 rules of *no handshaking*, withdraws his hand, and sits back down. 'What can I do for you detective?'

'We're here about one of your students...Bilal Mahmoud.'

Crawford's face clouds. 'What do you want to know?'

'Has he been attending school regularly, lately?'

'I would have to check on that.' He speaks into his intercom. 'Miss Waterford, can you get me the attendance list for Year 12.' Crawford looks to Ellington. 'What days are you interested in?'

'The last week or so,' Ellington replies. Crawford relays this to Miss Waterford. He rummages through a drawer and removes a file which he briefly studies before looking at his watch. 'Bilal's class would be in Room 7 right now.' Miss Waterford enters holding a clip file. She hands it to Crawford who studies each of the five pages before looking up with anxious eyes. 'Bilal Mahmoud has not attended school in the past ten days.'

Ellington and Sarah exchange glances. 'Does Bilal walk to school or does he drive? I noticed quite a few elderly cars parked in the area. I suspect a number of the senior students have access to cars.'

'Quite right. But I don't know too much about all that.'

Miss Waterford, who has lingered in the room, pipes up: 'Bilal Mahmoud does drive to school. You can't help but notice him…drives like a maniac, terribly dangerous,' she tut-tuts.

'What now?' Sarah asks as they pull away from the kerb.

'We come back tomorrow morning, and hope that Bilal leads us somewhere.'

*

That night Ellington stays again in Sarah's apartment. They have a cheap meal at the local pub and return for some television and an early night. Ellington reluctantly admits that sharing evenings with another human being has definite high points. But although he goes to bed relaxed and almost happy, the nightmares still come.

*

They leave the apartment early. The drive to Lakemba in rush hour traffic takes over an hour and they arrive in time to see a battered old Ford still parked in the front yard. They sit in silence, and at eight-thirty Bilal walks through the front door and out to the car. They follow him to the Hume Highway and head south-west.

'Miss Waterford wasn't kidding. That kid drives like a lunatic,' Sarah observes. Ellington's speedometer shows their travelling speed at one hundred and fifty kilometres an hour...well over the limit. Bilal slows down as they pass through the town of Camden. He stops in the main street and enters a supermarket. Fifteen minutes later he returns to his car carrying two bulging plastic bags. He sets off again but stays at a reasonable speed as he takes a back road on the outskirts of the town. Ellington follows at a distance and slows right down as Bilal stops his car outside a row of small factory-like buildings. He enters one of the buildings carrying the two plastic bags. Sarah and Ellington follow on foot. They both draw their pistols as they approach the half-opened doorway. They stop and listen. They hear Bilal's voice. 'The pillow and the sleeping bag are in the car. I'll go get them.'

Ellington and Sarah enter. Bilal is walking in their direction. His eyes bulge when he sees them. 'Hands up, Bilal' Ellington orders. Sarah darts past Bilal and moves quickly to the big swarthy man sitting on the floor. 'Hands up.' she shouts. Mohammed Marmoud throws his brother a filthy glare. 'You fucking half-wit,' he growls.

*

Ellington sits at the interrogation table next to Bellamy. Opposite are Mohammed Mahmoud and his lawyer. Sarah stands near the door. She studies Mahmoud's hard angry face, he looks older than his years. His dark eyes are heavy-lidded and his sallow swarthy skin sports a short black beard, there is no moustache. He wears a loose-fitting tracksuit and filthy sneakers.

Missing In Red

The lawyer's serious dark eyes are set beneath thick black brows. His clothing is impeccable...a dark grey business suit and a dazzling, crisp white shirt.

Bellamy goes through the preliminaries before launching into his interrogation. 'Mr Mahmoud, you are employed by New South Wales Corrective Services and work at Goulburn Correctional Centre. Correct?'

'Correct.' Mahmoud's voice is a low rumble and his eyes are cast down.

'In the course of your employment, did you come in contact with prisoner Campbell?'

'Yes.'

'On the morning of the first December, were you advised by Warden Richardson that you would be required to accompany prisoner Campbell in a police wagon to Goulburn Hospital?'

'Yes.'

'At what time were you given this information?'

Mahmoud sits with closed eyes. Thirty seconds pass before he speaks: 'About nine.'

At what time were you given the exact time of the proposed departure?'

'Later.'

'When?'

'An hour later.'

'So around ten, you were told the exact time of the proposed departure.'

'Yes.'

'And what time were you given?'

'Eleven.'

'So, you knew at ten that you would be leaving the prison at eleven?'

'Yes.'

'Did you mention this to any other prison officer or inmate?'

'I don't remember.'

'Did you speak to prisoner Campbell about this arrangement?'

'No.'

'Were you in the vicinity of prisoner Campbell between nine and the time you left the prison at eleven?'

'I might have been.'

'Did you talk with him?'

'No.'

There is a short pause while Bellamy consults his notes. 'So, when the police wagon arrived at the prison, what did you do?'

'The prisoner was put on a stretcher and carried to the wagon. The stretcher was put in the back of the wagon and I was instructed to sit in with the prisoner.'

'Was the prisoner cuffed?'

'Yes, I had cuffed him.'

'What happened then?'

'The two police officers who had driven the wagon in, got back into the front and drove out of the grounds.'

'What occurred during this journey?'

'We drove for about five or so minutes. Then the wagon stopped. There was talking in the front, I couldn't hear what was said. Then I heard two shots. A minute later the van door opened and I saw what I first thought was a policeman. He was holding a gun and ordered me out of the van. He then helped the prisoner out.' Mahmood looks up and there is a short silence before he continues. 'He told me to get into the police car that was parked just up in front. On the way, I saw the two policemen in the front of the wagon, both with bullet wounds. I said 'What's going on?' He pointed his gun at me and said '*get in the back.*' I got in the back of the car and the prisoner got in too. Then the prisoner said '*Get me out of these cuffs.*' I didn't know what was going on, so I just looked at the other guy. Then he said '*unlock them or I'll blast your head off.*' So, I unlocked the cuffs. Then the guy in the police suit gave the prisoner his gun and got in the driver's seat. We drove for a few minutes and then changed cars. Then we drove towards Sydney. The prisoner told the driver to drop me off at the Camden warehouse. He did, and I've been there ever since.'

'Mr Mahmoud, do you honestly expect us to believe that one of the most dangerous and vicious criminals in Australia dropped you off in perfect health after you had witnessed his accomplice murder two police officers?'

'That's what happened.'

'Why were you not killed like the others?'

'They were thinking of using me as a hostage.'

'And why did they change their minds?'

'I dunno. Campbell said somethin' about not really needing a hostage.'

'So, he just dropped you off?'

'Yeah.'

'You must take us all for half-wits if you think we'll swallow a cock and bull story like that.'

'Campbell owed me.'

Bellamy and Ellington exchange surprised glances.

'Owed you?'

'Yeah, I shared my cake with him.'

Sarah stifles a giggle. Bellamy makes a short guffaw. 'Well, that's something. What sort of cake was that, solid gold?'

'My mum sent me cakes and I gave some to Campbell. He really liked them.'

Bellamy shakes his head woefully. 'Campbell has an appetite for human flesh. It's news to me he likes cake.'

Ellington speaks slowly and deliberately. 'On your journey from Goulburn to Sydney, Campbell and his accomplice must have discussed Campbell's need for surgery. Tell us what was said.'

'He said something about seeing Dr Fixit.'

'Dr Fixit? That's the name he used?'

'Yeah.'

'Did either of them mention where Dr Fixit might be, or what was Dr Fixit's real name?'

'Nah.'

Bellamy officially terminates the tape after recording that bail will be robustly opposed.

Bellamy, Ellington, Sarah and Farrugia congregate in Bellamy's office. Bellamy speaks: 'There's no question, Mahmoud is lying. He's obviously an accomplice. He knew the exact time the wagon would be leaving the prison, and had an hour to alert the other accomplice. It's possible he doesn't have any worthwhile information about Campbell's present location, so we have to turn our attention back to Petrovic. I'll be applying for a warrant to search his place.'

'We've already searched,' Ellington says.

'How thorough were you?' Bellamy asks sarcastically.

Ellington nods, 'point taken.'

'Hopefully, that'll be happening tomorrow. I'd like all of you involved in that. I'll get Bonnington and Murray in too. It's a big house I'm told.'

'What about the other pseudo-medicos the crooks use?'

'There are three others in the State. I checked them out. One's in prison, one's dead and the third one's in a nursing home suffering dementia. It's possible that Campbell could have used a bona fide doctor, but at this point, Petrovic is the obvious culprit. There'll be no difficulty getting the warrant.'

'What did the surveillance guys have to say about Petrovic's movements?' Sarah asks.

'Not much. He walks his dog every day, goes shopping at the local Westfield, goes to the gym, plays golf, all very proper.'

*

'Like a drink?' Ellington asks Sarah as they leave the office.

'I've got lots in the fridge, let's have it at home.'

Sarah startles herself with what she said. If only she could take it back. She sounded like a wife!'

She turns on the ignition and with the flick of a switch the soft calming music of Enya fills the cabin. Ellington closes his eyes. 'I'm surprised you like this music, Sarah. I thought you'd be into rap or something.'

'How old do you think I am, fifteen?'

As they enter the apartment, Ellington says: 'It's my shout tonight. Feel like a meal at the local Italian?'

'Sounds good, I'm off for a shower, there's wine and beer in the fridge. Help yourself.'

As Ellington puts his hand around a Coopers beer, a blood-curdling scream cuts through the apartment. He drops the beer. At the bathroom door, he finds Sarah shaking violently, hands to her head, and still screaming. Hanging by its tail from the shower rose is a headless dog.

Ellington holds Sarah, turns her head to his chest, and softly pats his hand over her back. 'Shh,' he whispers. Her screams slowly dissolve into sobs.

Thirty minutes later, they are seated on the sofa sipping drinks. 'How did he find you? Could he have followed us?'

He shakes his head. 'No one followed us. I was watching.'

'Could he have put a tracker on your car?'

'When could he have done that?'

'He could have come back after he dumped the cat in your apartment that last night. How easy would it be for him to find your car in the parking area?'

'Pretty easy, I'll take a look,' he says thoughtfully.

Ellington goes down to the basement and inspects his car, and there it is! Campbell had planted a tracker. As he pulls the tracker off, Ellington reasons that Campbell had two days to track his car, break into Sarah's apartment and dump the dog.'

'I knew I should never have got you involved. It's one of my strictest rules. Never include others, especially family or friends.'

'What are you going to do?'

'I'll make sure you're safe. You must have a friend or a family member you can stay with?'

'And endanger them?'

'This'll be different. We'll make sure there are no trackers on your car, and we'll go now!'

'I can't just fall in on people.'

'Yes, you can.'

Two hours later Sarah drives out of the apartment and onto her married sister's house. Ellington follows her all the way. When he sees Sarah greeted at the front door, he turns and drives back to his apartment.

He pulls the heavy chest of drawers against the door and loads it with books. Any attempt at entry will definitely wake him. He makes himself a light snack and phones Sarah. 'You okay?'

'Yes. I'm settled in at Emma's, but I'll be going to bed

with my pistol under my pillow.'

'Good girl. Sorry about the Italian dinner, we'll have it soon. See you tomorrow.'

CHAPTER 21

Sarah and Ellington travel with Inspector Bellamy. The three other police travel in a second car. They arrive at Petrovic's house just as he is returning from walking his dog.

'What now?'

Bellamy hands Petrovic the warrant. 'A warrant to search these premises, unlock the door please.'

The dog growls as the six police walk past. 'I'll keep Rufus on his lead. He doesn't like cops.'

'Good idea,' mutters Sarah.

'Farrugia and I will take the front part of the house. Bonnington and Murray, you guys do the middle section and Duke and Bradley do the back and the garage. Be thorough.'

The back section of the house comprises the kitchen, family room and laundry. Ellington and Sarah work quietly and efficiently. After finding nothing of importance, they head out to the double garage. It contains only one car, a Porsche. A set of golf clubs and a battery-operated golf buggy stand in one corner, a wheelbarrow and various garden tools stand in another. Shelving around the room supports smaller tools, half-filled paint tins, car accessories and two small folding chairs. On exiting, Sarah stops suddenly and points. 'Look Luke, the interior of the garage finishes two, maybe two and a half metres shorter than the exterior.'

They go back inside and inspect the back wall which appears to be just a wall of fibrous cement panels. 'I think something might be behind this wall.' They both tap around the wall. A calendar hangs from the central panel. Sarah lifts it. An innocuous looking button is mounted on the wall. Sarah presses and the panel slides away revealing a long narrow room. An operating table stands in the centre of the room with a huge domed light hanging above. A large refrigerator stands on one wall and a tall steel cabinet on the other. 'Welcome to the operating room of Dr Fixit,' mutters Ellington as he opens the fridge. It contains sealed glass bottles and jars and packets of syringes. The cabinet contains surgical instruments, oxygen masks, iodine, bandages and plastic sheeting.

Bellamy confronts Petrovic. 'We found your operating room and are currently testing it for fingerprints. It is a criminal offence for an unregistered person to engage in medical procedures. What do you have to say?'

'I do not treat humans, only animals.'

'So, you are posing as a vet?'

'I only help people who can't afford to pay a vet. If it wasn't for me, many family pets would be put down. They know I'm not registered. I charge a pittance.'

'Well, if you charge a pittance, how do you explain this home, your Porsche?'

'The home belonged to my parents. I inherited it when they died. Apart from the house and the car, I have no other assets.'

*

'The only prints in that room belonged to Petrovic.' Bellamy absently shuffles papers on his desk.

'So, we've got nothing on him.'

'He was telling the truth about his assets, he's actually

254

on a Government Pension.'

'He could have squillions stacked away.'

'True, anyway we're continuing the surveillance. It's possible Campbell will call again on Petrovic for a check-up or whatever gets done after a gall bladder operation.'

'That reminds me sir, I feel I should ask for some protection. Campbell made death threats to me on the last day of his trial.' Bellamy straightens up, eyes wide. Ellington continues. 'Over the past few days someone has been twice to my apartment stringing up dead animals. I have reason to believe it was Campbell. I don't think there'll be any more dead animals. The next time, he'll be coming for me.'

'You should have told me about this before. Of course, you'll get protection, starting from tonight.'

Ellington throws his coat on the bed and winds open the hopper windows. An enormous full moon hangs in the sky illuminating the room. He sets the ceiling fans at full pace and silently admonishes himself for not having organised air conditioning. He had suffered through last summer's heat without it, and now, only in its early stage, this summer is promising to be hotter than the previous. He grabs his personal notebook and scribbles *organise air conditioning*. He pours himself a scotch and turns on the television. He thinks about eating and although hungry, feels almost too tired to cook anything.

A knock on the door sends his hand to the pistol which snuggles in the holster strapped across his chest. 'Who is it?'

'Constable Keith Willoughby, sent by Inspector Bellamy.'

Willoughby is tall and broad shouldered. A floppy mop of dark brown hair matches the tidy moustache which hovers above a mouth full of prominent teeth. Shaded glasses are perched across his wide nose. He shows his ID to Ellington.

'Come in, glad to see you. Hope you're ready for a long night because I'm ready for the sack. Take your coat off, sorry about the heat in here.'

'There's a nice breeze coming from them windows,' observes Willoughby.

'I meant to organise some air-conditioning, just haven't got around to it.' Ellington pokes into the fridge and finds some leftover spaghetti Bolognaise. 'Have you eaten constable?'

'Yes, thanks. My missus made a lovely leg of lamb. She knew I'd be out 'till morning. She looks after me real good, even packed a sandwich for later.' He holds up his rucksack.

'Half your luck mate, no leg of lamb here. Guess I'll have to settle for a heated-up spaghetti Bolognaise.'

Willoughby chuckles, 'nothing wrong with a good old Bol.'

Ellington heats up the Bolognaise and sits next to Willoughby while he eats. They watch a re-run of 'Lewis'. At ten, Ellington goes to the bathroom, brushes his teeth and heads for bed. He turns at the door. 'Help yourself to the coffee, there's soda and stuff in the fridge.'

'I'm fine mate.' Willoughby is still engrossed in the television which is now showing a re-run of 'New Tricks'.

'Don't forget you're looking after me, don't get too involved in the television.'

Willoughby laughs. 'Sleep tight mate. All's well.'

Ellington undresses, puts on his boxers and drifts off quickly. The dream is starting, but now there's something different. Usually, he doesn't see his attacker's face, but this time he sees Campbell. There he is with his chubby grand-daddy face, grey hair and cold pale eyes. The dream suddenly changes. Now Constable Willoughby is in the dream. He's got Ellington in a choking bear grip. The dark brown hair and moustache look wrong, they're at odds with the grey chin stubble. Ellington wakes and sits bolt upright. The door is opening slowly. The chink of light coming from the hallway widens, and combined with the strong moonlight, allows sufficient light for Ellington to see Keith Willoughby advancing toward him wielding an enormous hunting knife. He no longer wears glasses and even in the semi-light, the familiar icy eyes give away the disguise. Ellington springs from the bed. The knife is less than two metres away. There's no chance of getting to his pistol on the other side of the room. He grabs the small bedside table and using it as a shield, deflects the knife which crashes against it. In that instant, he lunges forward and using the anatomical knowledge gained from all those autopsies he's witnessed, stabs the metal leg of the table into the spot where Campbell's gall bladder once was. Ellington's rewarded with a growl of pain as the table leg hits its mark. Campbell, still wielding the knife moves in again for the strike. For a few seconds they spar, and then the knife is heading for Ellington's head. He raises the table and once again the knife is deflected. Ellington again jabs Campbell where now a circle of blood has seeped through. The force is sufficient to cause Campbell to lose balance. As he topples over, the knife falls from his grasp. Ellington lunges toward the cupboard and his pistol. As he passes Campbell, an iron arm grabs his ankle causing him to fall heavily. For a fleeting second, Ellington's eyes and the pale icy ones of his attacker are an arm's length apart. Ellington pulls himself to his knees and lands a forceful punch on Campbell's jaw. The punch sends the false nose, teeth and moustache flying off. Ellington lunges for the cupboard while Campbell writhes like a snake toward the knife. He grabs it and stands. The blood from his wound has now spread across his shirt. Ellington finds his firearm and turns to face the menacing knife. He takes aim and fires. It's a perfect hit, right in the centre of Campbell's forehead. For what feels like an eternity to Ellington, but in reality, is only a few seconds, Campbell remains standing, leering like a grotesque monster. Although Campbell was killed by the first shot, Ellington fires again and again until his victim finally crumples to the floor.

CHAPTER 22

Gregory Allenby has spent the entire morning trying to compose a suitable sermon for Sunday's service. He knows what they want to hear. Elise knew too, and she was able to come up with the goods. He's bluffed his way through the past few Sundays by parroting religious magazine articles instead of giving proper sermons. But now, some of the idiots are starting to make comments. His mind is numb and he wonders if it could have something to do with all the alcohol he's been consuming. His intake has grown considerably since coming to this boring place with its boring worshippers. Elise Seymour was the only bright light in a dull-as-dishwater community. He looks at his watch 'what the hell,' he mutters. He pulls a bottle of scotch from a desk drawer and pours himself a double nip. He takes a swig and goes back to his desk. The alcohol has further dulled his senses and there's no way he can get past the first line. Defeated and irritated, he closes down his computer, takes his scotch to the sitting room, and turns on the television. Within minutes, he's fast asleep.

It's late afternoon when he wakes, he's got a massive headache and considers some "hair of the dog". The clock tells him it's six—watering time. He's a creature of habit and unless it's raining, he religiously waters his garden around six each night.

He's deep in thought as the water drenches the straggly flowers in the front yard. He again tries to compose an appropriate first line for Sunday's sermon, but his mind is blank and nothing comes. Maybe he'll pretend his throat is bad. That worked before. No, they'd get suspicious. An idea brings relief. He'll go through some of Elise's old sermons. He's kept them all, just a few little changes, and no one will be the wiser. Most of the fools couldn't remember what they had for breakfast let alone a sermon they'd heard weeks ago. Yes, that's what he'll do. Moving on to the vegetable patch he fails to see the hooded figure enter through the far gate and hurry down the side path.

Allenby completes his task and goes to the letterbox to retrieve the day's mail. He sifts through the small pile. At the bottom is an envelope with no stamp, his name is written on the front in red block letters. He goes inside, pours himself a scotch, and opens the letter. There is a single page with words that at first make no sense, but on a second look, his body freezes. The words penned in bright red ink, jump out threateningly. *You Are Next. You must pay for Your Sins.* Allenby gulps, rushes to the wide opened front door and slams it shut. He knows what happened to Richard Ballantyne and Tara Gresham. His hands are shaking as he throws the scotch into the sink. He must keep his senses. He locks the back door, and on his way back to the sitting room, collects a two-iron from the golf bag in the bedroom. He sits at his desk with the club resting against the chair, and boots up the computer. He opens his Sermons file and selects one of Elise's sermons. As he reads it, his mind focuses on her and the last time she came.

He had been infatuated with the girl from the moment he first saw her, captivated by her innocent beauty, her soft voice, the beautiful clothes that covered her even more beautiful body. She was a devout Christian and initially made suggestions for his sermons. When he asked her for regular assistance, she agreed and offered to email him her ideas. He remembered the day he asked her to come to his home. He phoned her at the shop. *'Emailing them is fine Elise, but I need you here to discuss changes that could improve them. It really is the only way. Come around and I'll make you a nice dinner and then we can set to work after you finish at Maude Tingwell's.'*

'I'm sorry. I can't.'

'Why not?'

'I don't leave Maude until nine or so.'

'Why do you stay so long? You could fix her dinner and then come around here.'

'I don't know.'

'Elise, I need you. The parish needs you. I just can't seem to be able to deliver the sermons they want. You have the flair.' His voice took on authority. *'It's your duty.'*

'If you put it that way, I guess I have no option.'

'Good girl, but let's keep it our secret.'

'Why, Gregory?'

'You know how some old biddies like to gossip.'

On the nights Elise came, they started off with dinner. He prided himself on his cooking prowess and always made sure the dinners were above standard. Then they would go to the sitting room and discuss the coming sermon. After a few weeks, Elise protested.

'Gregory, there's really no need for me to come twice each week, once ought to do.'

*'There **is** need, Elise. I'm very lonely. You make my life special. Please. It's your duty.'*

As time went by, he occasionally made little intimate

remarks. There was never any response, but she kept coming, and he convinced himself that she was interested in him and was waiting. Then on that last day, the last time he saw her, he decided to make his move. He had deliberately poured extra-large glasses of wine during dinner and encouraged her to finish them. In the sitting room, he sat on the lounge and patted the seat next to him. She sat awkwardly. When he touched her, she moved slightly away from him.

'Elise, I have a confession to make.'

She looked at him with wide blue eyes.

'I love you and I want to make love to you.'

Elise moved away. 'No, Gregory, that's not on.'

He pulled her back towards him.

'What are you doing? Let me go.' Elise struggled. He was not going to back off. He couldn't. One hand was on her breast and the other finding its way up her skirt. 'Stop', she screamed.

'You stop. Stop struggling.' He slapped her hard across the face. She slumped backward and hit her head on the wooden arm of the chair. She lay there, dazed and semi-conscious. He pulled her to the floor and quickly removed her underwear. He was hard as a rock and wasted no time plunging his bulging penis into her. Suddenly her eyes snapped open. 'Stop, you're hurting me.' She tried to push him off. Using both hands he pinned her shoulders to the floor. Undeterred by her screaming he continued thrusting and pumping until he reached an explosive climax. He finally released his grip on her and rolled onto his back, sated and spent. Elise sobbed as she pulled herself up and gathered her underwear. As she stumbled away Allenby cried out, 'I love you, Elise. I love you.' The only response was the slamming of the front door.

Missing In Red

The memory of pumping into that tight little pussy arouses him again, and he responds with a full erection. Allenby shakes his head with guilt. Two days after that episode, she was gone. Was it because of what he'd done?

So aroused by his erotic thoughts, he doesn't hear the slight rustle behind him. Suddenly a tight wire is cutting into his throat. Pain and fear drench his body. He tries to pull the wire away, but it has a tight grip on his skin and is burrowing relentlessly. With a huge effort, he plants his feet on the floor and using his lower body, swivels the chair backward. He feels it hit his attacker. In that instant, the wire releases slightly, just enough for Allenby to get a better grip on it. Now it's cutting his fingers, slicing through the flesh. With his free hand, he reaches for the nearby golf club. Although still half-turned away from his assailant, he manages to swing the club backward making a glancing blow. As the club hits light clothing, the assailant's purchase on the wire is further loosened. With blood streaming from his left hand, Allenby pulls the wire from his neck. Now he can turn and face his enemy. The golf club is raised and this time he slams it into the hood. His attacker falls at his feet. The big hood is still covering the face. Allenby bends, pulls it aside and gasps, 'Oh my God.'

Allenby reaches for his phone and dials Emergency. 'I've been attacked. I need the police and an ambulance.' He looks at his victim and then at his hand. Blood is streaming from it, and now he sees drops running from his throat down his shirt. 'There are two injured, maybe two ambulances.'

CHAPTER 23

Janet Seymour is propped up with pillows. Her face is swollen and puffy, and the skin surrounding both eyes has turned blue-black. Her straight fair hair spreads lankly across the pillow. Ellington stands stiffly by the bed. Sarah is at the foot.

'Mrs Seymour, do you wish to make a statement about the attempted murder of Gregory Allenby and the murders of Richard Ballantyne and Tara Gresham?' Ellington's asks softly.

'Why not?' Her voice is thick and gravelly.

'Do you wish to have a solicitor present?'

'Not really.'

Ellington looks around for a power-point, finds one, and plugs in his recording device. He gives it a light tap to make sure it's working and sits beside the bed.

'Detective Sergeant Luke Ellington with Janet Seymour at the Prince Alfred Hospital on Friday morning the twenty-third December two thousand and twenty-one at'... he checks his watch 'two minutes past eleven. Senior Constable Sarah Bradley and Sergeant Geoffrey Murray are in attendance.' Ellington speaks slowly. 'I must warn you Mrs Seymour, that anything you say today can be used against you in a court of law. Do you wish to proceed?' He places the microphone close to her face.

'Yes.'

Ellington draws in his breath and continues. 'On the twenty-second November two thousand and twenty-one, Richard Ballantyne was standing on Summer Hill Railway station waiting for a train to convey him to Croydon. He was pushed from behind with such force that he fell beneath the oncoming train and was killed instantly. Did you push Richard Ballantyne?' Ellington moves the microphone close to Janet's mouth. There's an electric silence and then Janet whispers, 'I did, and I'll tell you why.' She pauses for a few seconds. 'He deserved to die for what he had done to Elise.'

'What had he done to Elise Seymour?'

'He broke her heart.'

Ellington glances across at Sarah who wears a disturbed frown. 'When did you decide to murder Richard Ballantyne?'

'The Monday after Elise went missing. I went to the pharmacy that morning. I wanted to talk to Catherine, find out everything Elise had said that last day. I had just parked my car when I saw him, Ballantyne. He was on his way to the station and whistling. Can you believe, whistling?' She eyeballs Ellington angrily. 'How dare he be happy after what he'd done to Elise. I followed him, watched him buy his paper, descend the stairs and walk to the top end of the platform. I noticed there was only one other passenger waiting in the area. The train came roaring in and that's when I made my plan.' A small smile plays around Janet's mouth as she recalls the events. 'For the next two mornings I followed him and the pattern was exactly the same.' She pauses and sighs. 'I had a bolt of grey material I'd bought for curtains, but never used, and I made the hooded cloak.' Janet reaches for the glass of water on her bedside table. She gulps some down and sinks her head back into the pillow.

'Go on.'

'I walked to the station that morning with my cloak under my arm. There's a small toilet block a few metres from the station's entrance. I went in, put on the cloak, and waited for him. I followed him down the stairs a minute or so after. I knew exactly where the CCTV cameras were, and turned my head away as I passed. I took a position further back from Ballantyne, and waited. I was lucky no one was nearby, just the usual fellow. He was standing a little forward of Ballantyne. I heard the train coming, and a second or two before it arrived, I hurled myself at him. I didn't wait to see the result, just hurried away before anyone even realised what had happened.' Janet closes her eyes. For a moment, Ellington thinks she's fallen asleep. Then she speaks again in a slow ordered voice. 'I knew I was taking an enormous risk. It all could have backfired. He might have resisted the push or someone could have seen me and grabbed me. I didn't care what happened, because my life was finished anyhow.' She reaches for the glass again and takes a tiny sip. 'I went into the toilet block, took off the cloak, and walked back home down Dixon Street.'

'So, you are admitting that you had pre-planned the murder of Richard Ballantyne. Is that correct?'

'Yes.'

Ellington exchanges a quick glance with Sarah and speaks again into the microphone. 'On the twenty-ninth of November two thousand and twenty-one, Tara Gresham's throat was cut in the garage of her home. She died at the scene. Did you kill her?'

'She deceived Elise. She was a traitor.'

'Did you kill Tara Gresham?'

'Yes.'

Missing In Red

'Tell me how you killed Tara Gresham.'

Janet's eyes search the ceiling as she speaks. 'Elise and Tara had worked together. I knew all Tara's little habits, like Thursday nights she always goes for a night on the town straight from work. Elise used to be a part of the group and she and Tara would share the driving home, whoever felt the best able to drive. I had keys to Tara's car. Elise had sold it to her previously but had kept a set of keys. I knew the car would be in the building's basement parking. I waited in the back seat for Tara to come. I had intended killing her there and then, but some people turned up and I had to change my plan. It was quite uncomfortable lying on the floor. I had to be quiet and patient. When she pulled up in her garage, I killed her. It was really quite easy and I had the bonus of a free trip home.'

Ellington is disgusted at the woman's tone. It's as if she was talking about killing an ant. A faint breeze rattles the blinds breaking the deadly silence that has settled in the room. Ellington speaks again: 'On the twenty-second of December two thousand and twenty-one, Gregory Allenby was attacked in his home with the same weapon that killed Tara Gresham. He survived the attack with deep cuts to the neck and hand. Did you attempt to kill Gregory Allenby?'

'Yes. I'm sorry I failed there. He deserved to die, but I *did* hurt him,' she smiles.

'Why did Allenby deserve to die?'

'He defiled Elise, he raped her.'

'How did you know that Allenby was the rapist?'

'Elise told me.'

'You never disclosed that.'

'No, I didn't.

'Why?'

'I had my reasons.'

There is a strained silence before Ellington asks: 'Where is Elise Seymour?'

Janet's eyes flit around the room. Finally, they close and she whispers: 'She's dead.'

Ellington feels a wave of emotion sweep over him. He battles to retain his composure.

'Did you kill her?'

'Of course not, I loved my daughter, she was my whole world.' Janet's eyes remain closed.

'What happened to her?'

Janet's eyes snap open, and her face contorts in anger. 'She killed herself, because of those three people. They drove her to it. Their guilt is as real as if they'd actually poured those pills down her throat. They had to pay.'

'Where is your daughter's body?'

'I was protecting her image. To the church people, Elise was a saint.' Janet smiles sadly. 'Many of them hold extreme conservative views on the bible and its interpretations, and many believe suicide is a sin. I wanted Elise to be remembered as the beautiful young girl they'd put on a saintly pedestal.'

'Where is Elise?' Ellington's voice is harsh as he repeats the question.

'In the rose garden, that's where I buried her.'

Ellington is feeling his own personal pain as he says: 'Mrs Seymour, in your own words, say exactly what happened on fifteenth November two thousand and nineteen.'

Janet takes a deep breath. 'That morning started just like any other morning. David was still in Canberra and I got up at my usual time. At seven, I knocked on Elise's door. *Time to get up,* I called. There was no answer. I thought she must have been in the shower. Twenty minutes later, Elise hadn't appeared for breakfast and I went back to her room and knocked again. *Elise?* I called. There was no answer so I opened the door and saw her still in bed. At first, I thought she had just slept in. Don't know why I thought that. Elise never slept in, not since she broke with Ballantyne and his crowd. She lay there, so quiet and peaceful. I touched her face, it was cold. My heart and soul were ripped into shreds in that instant. My beautiful daughter was dead. There was an empty pill bottle nearby and a letter. It was a long time before I could bring myself to read that letter. I sat with her and kissed her cold cheeks and ran my hand through her lovely hair. I was numb with grief. Eventually, I read her letter. I've read that letter every day since. Without looking at it, I can tell you every word.' Janet looks at Ellington. He nods. She continues in a low soft voice. *Dear Mum and Dad please forgive me for this, but my life is just not worth living. I have suffered terribly since Rick left me and all I wanted was to have him back. When Tara called last night saying that she and Rick were over, I was elated. My fervent dreams were coming true. My darling Rick was returning to me. I met him this morning, thinking he would be begging me to come back to him, but my world was shattered. He told me he wasn't interested in me and was going overseas. He was quite brutal and spared me nothing. I spent the whole day deciding what to do. The dispensary is full of avenues of release, and I took one. It's not all about Rick. I had been writing Gregory Allenby's sermons and going there Tuesdays and Fridays. He said it was my duty. And then on Tuesday night, he raped me. That is just another reason why I have to go. My life is over...Elise.'*

Janet opens her eyes and takes a deep breath. 'I was in deep shock but pulled myself together and thought and thought. Finally, I came to a decision. At nine I took the phone off the hook. I didn't want the chemist or anyone else, calling.

I needed solitude to do what I had to do. I went to the rose garden and started digging. It was hard work but I'm quite strong.' She gives a mirthless chuckle. 'All those years of competitive sailing, gave me strong hands and wrists.' She looks down at her hands and sighs. 'That girl from the pharmacy came around while I was digging, I heard her call at the side gate. I was relieved when she went away. It took me nine hours. Finally, it was done. I went inside and dressed my darling girl in her new red dress and black shoes. I wrapped her in a sheet and dragged her through the house and down to the rose garden. The hardest part of all was covering my beautiful girl with dirt.' She looks steadily at Ellington. 'I did forget the joggers though. You were quite the clever detective about those, weren't you?'

'Elise's mobile was found on Douglas Street. How did it get there?'

'I planted it there early the next morning. I wanted to make it look as if Elise had dropped it while being abducted.'

'Where is Lisa's suicide letter?'

'It's in the family bible, Corinthians, the verse on suicide.'

'Does your husband know any of this?'

'Nothing, I had to protect him too. Political careers don't thrive well if there's a suicide in the family.' She offers a crooked smile.

Janet glances at Ellington and then at Sarah. She sighs heavily and closes her eyes. 'Elise was my only child. She was everything to me. She was pretty, caring, intelligent, and then she fell for that creep, Ballantyne. We tried to warn her, but she took no notice. He dumped her for that empty-headed scheming bitch, Tara Gresham. That was the beginning. Elise was inconsolable. She loved the man, and in a way, she loved Tara her best friend, but both betrayed her. Her pain was awful. I understood it, even though Elise didn't confide in me. She gave up a promising career and became a sales assistant. I thought she was coming to terms with it all when she became involved in the church. She gave so much of herself to that. She did charitable works, helped elderly parishioners, she even helped Allenby with his sermons, and then the bastard raped her.'

Ellington frowns and his tone is sharp and bitter. 'Janet Seymour I am arresting you for the murders of Richard Ballantyne and Tara Gresham and for the attempted murder of Gregory Allenby. You are also charged with illegally disposing of the body of your daughter, Elise Seymour.'

Stepping out in the sunlight, Sarah is concerned by Ellington's fierce expression. 'She's a monster,' he mutters.

'Calm down Luke, she'll get her punishment.' They walk in silence to the car.

'What about that girl up in Sea Haven?' Sarah asks.

'Just a good look-alike apparently.'

Ellington manoeuvres the car through the city traffic. He looks sideways at Sarah, 'I'll drop you back at the station. I have to go to the Seymour place and pick up that suicide note.'

'If the bible was in with her other books, I don't know how I missed it,' Sarah murmurs.

CHAPTER 24

When there's no response to his knocking, Ellington walks around the side to the back garden. David Seymour is sitting under a shady tree. He looks up surprised. 'Detective!'

'Mr Seymour, I've just come from the hospital.'

'Has Janet regained consciousness?'

'She has'. Ellington draws in a deep breath. He releases it slowly. 'Your wife has confessed to the attempted murder of Gregory Allenby and the murders of Richard Ballantyne and Tara Gresham.'

David Seymour rubs a hand across his forehead. 'Oh my God, you must be mistaken.' He stands shakily.

Ellington puts out a steadying hand. 'Let's go inside, I'll get you some water.'

The kitchen is bright and cheerful. Seymour reaches into a high cupboard and withdraws a whisky bottle. I don't think water is quite what I need. Can I pour you one?'

'No thanks.'

Seymour pours a good measure, downs it in one long gulp, plonks the bottle on the kitchen table and sits heavily. 'I knew she was devastated over Elise's disappearance, but I didn't realise she'd lost her mind. Could there be a mistake, about Ballantyne and the girl, I mean? I know she was at Allenby's place and tried to hurt him but the other two? How is she supposed to have killed Ballantyne? I thought he went under a train.'

'She pushed him.'

'It seems absurd. What about the girl?'

'Your wife hid in Tara Gresham's car and strangled her with wire. Did you suspect anything at all?'

'No. The night she attacked Allenby, she said she was going for a walk.' He pours another hefty shot.

'The night she killed Tara she must have been missing quite a while. Where did you think she'd gone?'

'I would have been in Canberra that night. Parliament was still sitting.'

Ellington's expression is grave. 'I have something else to tell you. I'm afraid it's very bad news.'

Seymour looks at Ellington with hang-dog eyes and swallows the shot.

'Your daughter is dead.'

Seymour's mouth opens and his face seems to collapse. His voice is barely audible. 'Janet would never hurt Elise,' he whispers.

'Elise committed suicide. I'm very sorry.'

'Where is she?'

'Your wife buried her in the rose garden.' He nods his head towards the backyard. 'Mr Seymour, I need to take possession of Elise's suicide note. I understand it's in the family Bible. Could you find me the Bible please?'

'It's in Elise's room.'

'May I get it?'

Seymour nods.

Ellington is once again in the hauntingly beautiful room. He breathes in the perfumed air and feels an intense sadness. He runs his hand across the soft pink bedspread and remembers his incredible dream. He goes through the books.

The Bible is not there. That would explain why Sarah didn't find it. He searches through the wardrobe and is about to give up when he goes back to the bed and lifts the mattress. The Bible is sandwiched between the base and the mattress. He sits on the bed, opens the book at the marked page, and retrieves the letter. He immediately recognises the small rounded writing. Janet Seymour had accurately recited Elise's letter word for word. Before closing the Bible, his eye catches the verse underlined in red: *Do you not know that you are God's Temple and that God's Spirit dwells in you? If anyone destroys God's Temple God will destroy him, for God's Temple is holy and you are that Temple.*

He never saw or spoke with Elise, yet he was intrigued by her. It was almost as if he'd been involved with her in a previous life. He goes to the record cabinet and finds the Nat King Cole record. He turns it over in his hand and makes a decision.

David Seymour is back in the yard, sitting on a bench near the rose garden. The roses are in bloom and the perfume is sweet.

Seymour looks up as Ellington arrives. 'Did you find it?'
'I did.'
'May I see it?'
'Of course,' Ellington hands him the letter. Seymour reads it and then hands it back. He buries his head in his hands and his shoulders heave as huge sobs shake his body. 'She was such a beautiful girl.'
'Yes, she was.'
'What will happen to Janet?'
'She will come to trial.'
'Can we plead insanity? She wasn't well, you know.'
'No, I didn't know.'
'It was a familial thing. Her own father committed

suicide. He had a mental problem, and Elise, too. But Janet would never admit to being ill, she never took medication.'

'Well, if it can be proven, it will certainly make a difference.'

'Hospital for the criminally insane, or gaol,' Seymour smiles cynically. 'I wonder which is the lesser of two evils.'

'What will you do?"

'I will quit politics and leave this area. My life is finished too.' He searches in his pocket, finds a handkerchief and blows his nose. 'When will they come...to dig her up?' He nods towards the garden.

'Soon, I expect, maybe tomorrow. I'll make sure you're informed beforehand.'

'I wonder if you would mind my taking this.' Ellington holds up the record. 'It was in Elise's collection. If you want to keep it, I understand.'

'Please take it Sergeant, there's a lot of other memorabilia in that room.'

*

Ellington and Sarah stand stiffly as two men dig in the rose garden. 'I'm surprised they didn't bring in machinery for this,' says Sarah.

'Janet Seymour said the grave was fairly shallow. We thought equipment mightn't be necessary.'

A shout from one of the diggers alerts them. 'I've got something.'

Ellington walks slowly to the garden and looks into the grave. At first, all he sees is a white sheet covering the top half of Elise's body. He allows his eyes to travel down to where the sheet has fallen away. The bright red material finishes just above her knees and black court shoes are still on her feet. Something catches in his throat, and he walks away.

Sarah sees his grim expression. 'Didn't think you'd be bothered by a dead body, Luke,' she says softly.

His voice is harsh. 'I've seen dozens of dead bodies.'

Sarah feels Ellington's torment but says nothing. They stand silently together as Elise is lifted from the grave. Ellington approaches David Seymour who is looking grey and unsteady. 'Are you able at this time to identify Elise, sir? I'm afraid we will need formal identification.'

Seymour nods and approaches the body. Ellington hears the quiet voice. 'Yes, that's Elise. That's my daughter.'

Sarah looks sideways at Ellington as he pulls away from the kerb. 'You okay Luke?'

Ellington ignores the question. 'We have business with Pastor Allenby, might as well go there now seeing we're in the area.'

'He's out of hospital?'

'Discharged this morning.'

As they arrive at the house, they see Allenby walk to the car parked in the driveway. He's dragging a large wheeled suitcase.

'We might be just in time,' Ellington mutters. He drives up the driveway, blocking Allenby's exit.

Allenby looks at them with surprise and concern. A huge bandage covers his left hand and a smaller one encircles his throat.

'Going somewhere, parson?'

'Just having a little break up the coast, I've been to hell and back these past few days.'

'I'm afraid you might have to postpone your little break, sir. I'm arresting you for the rape of Elise Seymour on the thirteenth of November. I warn you that anything you say could be used against you in a court of law. Are you coming quietly, or do we have to handcuff you?'

Allenby splutters. 'I'm not guilty. They're all liars, all

fucking liars.'

'In the car please.' Ellington guides Allenby to the car and pushes him into the back seat.

*

That night Sarah and Ellington visit the local tavern. 'I'm having champagne tonight and it's my shout,' Sarah says with mock severity. She gets the drinks at the bar, slides into the bench seat next to Ellington, and raises her glass. 'Cheers,' she takes a sip. 'What a time you've had.'

'What a time.' Ellington raises his glass and clinks it with Sarah's.

'How did Campbell find out about Officer Willoughby and the protection?'

'Campbell's criminal life netted him a small fortune, most of it's still out there. No one knows where it is or who is looking after it. It could be in a box in someone's cellar or it could be in a hundred bank accounts under a hundred different names.' Ellington takes a sip of his drink. 'He had accomplices all over the country from all different walks of life...lawyers, bank managers, accountants, motel owners, car dealers, prison officers and policemen. You name it. They were all willing to sell their souls for a piece of Campbell's stash.'

'Someone must have been looking after it while he was in prison.'

'Undoubtedly.'

'Well, there's a traitor in the Force apparently.'

'Campbell knew Willoughby was from a suburban station and played on the likelihood that I didn't know him, but of course, he had to use a disguise even so.'

'You knew Campbell well. I'm surprised you didn't see through the disguise.'

'I had never really seen him up close. I saw him at the

trial of course but then, he was sporting a big gut. Prison life had obviously trimmed him right down. The false nose, teeth, moustache and wig really altered the look of him, plus the built-up shoes. The only things about Campbell I would have recognised, were his eyes. I'd never seen eyes like that before. But that night he'd covered them with shaded glasses. What I missed and shouldn't have, was the grey stubble on his chin. It didn't match the brown moustache. My subconscious picked it up and warned me in a dream.'

'He went to all that trouble with his disguise, but forgot to shave his chin.' Sarah sips her wine. 'When did they find Officer Willoughby?'

'The next morning, he was stuffed in a council bin in Ryde.'

'Campbell could have used Constable Willoughby's firearm rather than a knife. The outcome might have been different.'

'Campbell always kills with a knife. It's his trademark.'

'What will happen to Mahmoud?'

'Most likely he'll be convicted.'

'And Petrovic?'

'We don't have anything on him, he won't be charged.'

They finish their champagne and Ellington says: 'Now how about that Italian dinner I promised you?'

*

The sun is setting and the glittering harbour is shot with shafts of pink and orange. Their table commands a splendid view, and they quietly watch the myriad of sailing boats gliding by.

'Did you suspect that Elise was dead?' Sarah asks.

'Not at first.'

'She was such a pretty girl, but so complicated.' Sarah sips her wine.

'I think the mother had a lot to do with that.'

'Do you think Janet Seymour's insane?'

'Not sure. I don't think a plea of insanity will stick, but we'll have to wait and see.'

The short silence is broken by Sarah. 'You seemed upset when they dug her up.'

Ellington shrugs and drains his glass.

'I think she got to you.'

'She was a total enigma.'

'I'm sorry I missed the Bible. If I'd found the suicide letter, things might have been different.'

'You didn't miss it. It wasn't with her other books. Janet Seymour had hidden it under the mattress.'

'That's such a relief.'

'That room had such an atmosphere. I could almost feel her there.'

'She died there.'

'Yes.'

'You never told me how you knew all that fifties stuff.'

Ellington smiles, 'my grandmother told me. The fifties were her special years.'

'What will happen to Elise's beautiful dresses?'

'I didn't think you liked them.'

'Well, quite coincidentally, that fashion seems to have been resurrected. It's all the rage.'

'Would you like one?'

'I'd love the dark pink one.'

Ellington recalls Elise's diary entry. 'The watermelon pink one?'

'Watermelon pink, yes I guess the pink was the colour of a watermelon. Do you think David Seymour would sell it to me?'

'You can only ask. It might be a bit long for you though.

Elise was a tad taller than you.'

She smiles. 'I'm rather handy with a needle and thread.'

'So many talents,' he grins.

Sarah raises her glass, 'To you Luke for solving this case.'

'The case really solved itself. I think Janet Seymour wanted to be caught. Why warn her intended victims?'

'True.'

Ellington fills both glasses and raises his. 'A toast to you Sarah Bradley, you're on your way to becoming a top detective.'

'Me?'

'You showed great bravery offering me sanctuary when Campbell came after me. You could have lost your life.'

Sarah shakes her head.

'And you showed incredible initiative when you investigated Brown's house,' he smiles teasingly.

Sarah giggles. 'You didn't call it initiative at the time.'

'And you found Petrovic's operating room. *I* missed that.'

'I'm feeling embarrassed,' Sarah says quietly.

'It won't go unnoticed. I'll be in Bellamy's ear tomorrow.'

'You can't. Tomorrow's Christmas,' Sarah smiles.

'So it is. What are you up to?'

'I'll undoubtedly spend it with my parents, my sister and my nephews. What about you?'

'I'll undoubtedly spend it with my parents and my beautiful grandmother down Wollongong way.'

'Will you stay over with them?'

'No fear, I'll be shooting through straight after the plum pudding.'

'Are you planning anything for Boxing Day?'

'I thought I'd check out the waves at Bondi. What about you?'

'I was thinking the same thing. I was also thinking about how nice those fish and chips were.'

'Sounds like a great day.'

'I can hardly wait.'

Ellington reaches across the table and takes Sarah's hand.

*

That night he has another vivid dream. He's back in the pink clouds and he's dancing again to the sound of beautiful music. He's holding her tightly and she's wearing the watermelon pink dress, but this time it isn't Elise he's holding, it's Sarah.

ACKNOWLEDGEMENTS

Thanks to my daughter, Lisa for allowing me to use her photo for the book's cover.
Thanks to my good friend Brian Hodges for proofreading the draft copy.

Missing In Red

Thank you for reading "Missing in Red". If you have time, I would appreciate a review or rating of this novel.

www.ingramcontent.com/pod-product-compliance
Lightning Source LLC
Chambersburg PA
CBHW030239030426
42336CB00009B/168